Our First Ten Days

The Birth of Christian Faith

Leonard Woodson Mann

CSS Publishing Company, Inc.
Lima, Ohio

OUR FIRST TEN DAYS

FIRST EDITION
Copyright © 2013
by CSS Publishing Co., Inc.

Library of Congress Cataloging-in-Publication Data

Mann, Leonard W.
    Our first ten days : the birth of christian faith / Leonard W. Mann.
        pages cm
    ISBN 0-7880-2732-8 (alk. paper)
    1. Apostles. 2. Jesus Christ--Disciples. I. Title.

    BS2440.M33 2013
    226'.0922--dc23

                                                        2013010307

For more information about CSS Publishing Company resources, visit our website at www.csspub.com, email us at csr@csspub.com, or call (800) 241-4056.

ISBN-13: 978-0-7880-2732-1
ISBN-10: 0-7880-2732-8   PRINTED IN USA

In deep gratitude, I am remembering a great many good people of this Discipleship, a few yet living but most gone on, who have, through all my many years, at various times and in numerous ways, guided, encouraged, motivated, and inspired me. I am thankful that, years ago, these embraced and welcomed me, and that, ever after, they have believed in and trusted me, and helped to keep me going. To all these I dedicate this book.

Introduction

An intriguing canvas from a master painter hangs on a gallery wall. Of course, only a few ever see it, although there are many who pause to look and then pass on by. Suppose, however, that this masterpiece was anciently damaged in a tragic fire and that a significant area in the midst of it was burned away. Today, whoever would seek to see the painting must at least try to visualize what once was in that empty space. A normal aesthetic sensibility virtually requires this of any who will attempt the seeing. Something belongs in that place, and to see the painting whole, the viewer must do his very best to discover what that is.

In his search, only this he knows: the key to what is lost, if there is one, may be found only in what remains. Therefore, he will linger long and ponder well.

The New Testament portion of the Holy Bible stands as a masterpiece in the library of world literature. This ancient book is a magnificent narrative, a story. It tells us about the life of Jesus and events in the lives of certain others at that time and for a short while afterward. It reports or describes many hundreds of happenings — speeches made, letters written, journeys made, sins forgiven, lessons learned, lives changed, and much more. Altogether, the story is a linked chain of events about a century long, telling us virtually everything we know of how Christianity began.

There are, however, vacant spaces in this story, links missing from the chain, segments of time during which we may long to know what happened, but are not told. One of these is a period of rare importance, a really momentous time: those first ten days after the last time the disciples saw Jesus. Please try with me to visualize that time, try to imagine the storms of perplexity and perhaps anxiety that must have torn at those people then.

The apostles and other disciples of Jesus, having known him for three years, probably thought they knew him fairly well. They had not, however, expected a crucifixion, and even less a resurrection. Afterward their crucified leader, alive, appeared to greet them, to stand among them, and to speak with them. Then suddenly he was gone, his parting words: "Wait here in Jerusalem."

Obediently, faithfully, they waited. For what? They did not know, could not know; they had no precedent for knowing. And there would be ten days of the waiting. These were ordinary common folk, normal Palestinian people; theirs were ordinary human minds. How would you have handled all of that? I am not sure that I could have. How did they? We are not told. There is perhaps a small item concerning a replacement for Judas; nothing more, nothing.

Most recently, walking with Jesus somewhere along the Bethany Road, these devoted followers of his suddenly found themselves alone, alone to ponder the mystery of him. With this final episode, the evidence concerning Jesus was now all in place, the data was all in hand. What could these people do with it? And what would they?

You and I have had 2,000 years to consider it. Those disciples, as their waiting time began, had less than 24 hours. Here they were, standing face-to-face with most awesome events, events unlike any ever known before. What to make of these events, what to make of this man — such were the questions. To take the raw data and try to find the meaning of it — this was their task.

In doing the things he did, what had Jesus done? And now these disciples, orphaned as they were, what should they do? Three years with Jesus now past, was this the end? Or did something await, and if so what? Ten days and ten nights, and it is doubtful if ever, before or after, has the human mind been put to greater task or spirit to deeper test.

So what, do you suppose, happened among those people

during those ten days? Surely there were great questions that needed answering. Beyond this, perhaps there were interpersonal tensions that called for resolution. We may be reasonably certain that those days were not spent in casual conversation about weather or fishing or the olive harvest! Afterward, philosophers and scholars would spend centuries trying to understand Jesus and to hammer the Christian Faith into some kind of shape. They would take that process past Nestorious and Arius and through Nicaea and Chalcedon. Here, though, for ten critical days the whole burden of the mystery would lie heavily upon a small band of witnesses who surely must have struggled beneath the weight of it. The Christian Faith had not leaped full-grown into life on resurrection morning or ascension day. When divine things had been divinely done, there was much left for human doing.

And they to whom the task would first fall were these nearest the scene and most involved with the strange matters concerning Christ. These had now gathered, and of their agenda we have no record. For the listening ear, we have only silence, and for the searching eye, nothing. We may be sure, however, that things happened and things of the recent past were deeply considered, reviewed, pondered, and probed for meaning. Specifically, what happened and what was said among those people? Of course, I do not know, nor can I ever know. But I stand entranced before all this as though before that master painting with the missing part, trying hard to visualize the completion of the master painter's art.

And I do know this: The key to what is lost, if there is one, may be found only in what remains. Therefore I began, more than 75 years ago, to explore the scriptural record of time-before and time-after, seeking to learn all I might about the people involved and the circumstances into which they had been thrust. The result has been for me the blessing of lifelong Bible study, and for any who may read it, the creation of this book, a tentative small story, offered as commentary upon the greatest story ever told.

Now, a suggestion —
To you, my dear reader: When you have read to the end of this book, you may feel that what I have written is way off target. Maybe it is. Who knows? Who will ever know? But I think we do know this: among those people in those days things did happen. Can you even imagine that those scores of disciples sat around looking at one another, doing nothing, saying nothing? If this book fails to offer a satisfying scenario, I suggest, urge really, that you develop your own. Put your mind to a challenging and exciting task; do your own studies and create your own story. No, you may not have 75 years to work on it! But you will find the time well spent and especially the project extremely rewarding.

I

One of the Twelve strongly advised that I not speak of this, and I have therefore kept long silence. The day of my life, however, is now well past its noon and the sunset is in view. While memories of the dawn still linger, I think I must say what I have seen. Besides, circumstances have changed. With the passing of these years, the reasons for my silence have largely ceased to be. I believe that the apostle would not now hold me bound by the promise I made then.

Perhaps you wonder that the silence was imposed upon me. At the time I wondered also, but did not question. As I have pondered the matter, I think I may know the reason. It lies possibly in one of the most common emotions of any man: Some experiences are too precious or too personal to be put on parade, some inner movements of spirit, signaled as they are by deed and word, are too much one's own to be laid bare before any other. At least I think this was in the apostle's thought that day when he put his arm around me, drew me close to him, and said the thing he did.

Now, you are party to this Faith. You have a right to know, and, I think, should know in what way it all began, the travail that gave it birth, the sledge blows that hammered the hot metal into the shape it is, the struggles that took the great fact and from it formed and shaped this Faith.

Of all who were there, I am one of only a few who are left. I was young then, youngest of them all. Since word now comes from Ephesus that John is dead, I believe that only Jarrod and Milcus remain.

I was there from the start, a kind of errand boy I suppose, going on small missions for the group, carrying a message to someone away or running to the baker's or the candlemaker's. Sometimes it was I who watched at the door, and sometimes I only sat and listened.

Because I was so young, they scarcely thought of me as privy to it all. Not until it was over. It was after the great excitement that Bartholomew seemed to see me as though for the first time, and it was then that he strictly charged me to cherish in heart all I knew, but never to reveal it to anyone.

I have kept the confidence, nor would I breach it now. I think, however, if Bartholomew or any of the others could speak with me, they would say, "Our people have their right to know." Therefore I speak.

Thaddaeus was my uncle. And this is how it was I entered the room at the first. Passing on the street and seeing me standing there, he beckoned and bade me fetch a thing he required and meet him at the room. This I did. And there being others who needed things and therefore needed me, there I stayed, as I say, in and out, for the whole of the ten days.

I had last seen my uncle at the Olivet Gate, where he and the company, forty or fifty in number, had walked from the city on the road that leads to Bethany. Jesus had been with them; there was no question about that. I had seen him two or three times on previous occasions and had no doubt that this was he.

Earlier, he had worn the usual road garments of Galilee, but this day he was clothed in a robe of exquisite white and seemed to stand somewhat taller than before. He had walked at the forefront of the company, two or three close by on either side. I had watched their descent into the Kidron and had seen them climb toward the mount beyond.

Here at the gate I had waited, and here it was, when the party returned, that my mother's brother saw me standing. Jesus was not with them now and apparent amongst them was much distress and perplexity. Some wept, some were silent, but most talked in groups of threes or fours. Their voices low, speaking in whispered tones really, their words

I was unable to hear. Some turned from time to time, gazing back across the valley. I marveled why.

At length all were past the gate and into the city again. It was now my uncle spoke with me.

Fifteen or twenty were in the room when I arrived, Thaddaeus among them. All were silent, nor, I think, had any spoken since entering there. The same silence fell on me. Quietly, I slipped into a corner near the door, and there I waited, sitting quite still on the flagstone floor. Others came, in equal silence entering.

The time was well near evening, about the ninth or tenth hour I would say. Bright rays of sun, steeply slanted, streamed through the westward windows, making geometric patterns on the floor. The lamps had not been lit and the far corners were shadowed somewhat. A great table stood at one end, a few chairs were scattered about, three stone jars stood in one corner, and there was little else.

This was an upper room, very large, and alongside it a rooftop terrace almost as large as the room itself. The one doorway opened onto this and a single stair ascended from the street. Up this stair, on sandaled feet, the disciples came slowly, stepping softly. Apprehensively, they approached the room, and, as I have said, silently they entered it.

Great questions leaped from their eyes, and sometimes it seemed these were framed on their lips but never phrased. Sometimes friend glanced to friend and then suddenly turned away. Some looked long and searchingly into the faces of those nearby.

Once a huge man sitting alone at the table's most shadowed end, face buried in folded arms, lifted his shoulders heavily, gazed upward as into space, and sighed so audibly many heard. One nearby stepped over a pace and lightly laid a hand on the man's shoulder. There was then something like a sob and all was quiet again.

It was a long while before I heard a voice. The voice I

then heard I think was that of James, the older of the two. I had never heard his voice before, although I did many times thereafter; and in the dim light I was unable to see the man whose voice arose somewhere in the midst.

James was a large man, his voice by nature strong, but now the tones were soft, whispered almost. But they were the tones of James, I am sure, and soft, I think, for the same reason that he softly speaks who is first to break the silence of a temple.

"I... do not... understand..." The words came slowly, incredulously. A wave of motion moved across the room as disciples turned to the speaker, eager for what he might next say. But he said nothing, not for a long while. Then he repeated, "I do not understand; I cannot understand it at all. What is the meaning of it?"

There was no reply and a long silence followed. The day was nearing twilight before another person spoke. It was Thomas then who spoke to one near him, "Andrew, do you think he will come?"

The response was an immediate surge of motion about the room as all turned to face the speaker. For a long while Andrew made no reply. Then, after a deep breath and a long sigh, he said, inaudibly almost, "I don't know."

Another spoke, "He told us to wait."

The Eleven began now to gather from their several places and to assemble near the center of the room. Soon eight or nine were there.

One said, "We believed we had seen him the final time the day he died. But not so. We know this now."

Other voices entered and most I heard:

"May he not come to us again?"

"He has come before."

"Will he, though?"

"Suppose he does not, what then?"

"And suppose he does?"

"If he comes, what will he do?"

"And if he does not come, what will we do?"

"He said we should wait." This was the same voice I had heard before.

From his place at the shadowed end of the table the huge man slowly arose, his bulk seeming almost to diminish the size of the room. As most eyes turned toward him, so did mine. Seeing more clearly now, the man I saw I knew to be Simon, the fisherman from Galilee.

In an awed voice Simon said, "Once before, he met us at this place. He sat at this table, this very table. Some of our number were with him here..." The voice faded into silence. Then the big man breathed deeply as if to go on, but nothing came. He turned wearily and took again his place at the table.

After a short while, another spoke: "My mind goes back to a thing that happened here. The way he broke the bread for us at table that night — do any remember?"

"Yes," someone replied, "he said, 'This is my body.' Something strange there was in the way he said that."

Among this central cluster of apostles, no one spoke for a while, each of the men seemingly preoccupied with his own thoughts and memories. Then one said, "He spoke of his body as a man might speak of any possession, an ass or a staff perhaps."

"Or a cloak," said one, Thomas, I think.

Then another added, "A garment? Yes. It may be worn or laid aside. Is this the meaning?"

All this transpired in an air of awe, the voices subdued, hesitant, tentative. Around the perimeter of the room the assembled followers strained to hear what was being said at the center. From one side, one of the women spoke, her voice quavering: "Where is he now?"

A long silence was then broken by the son of Alphaeus, repeating, "Where is he now? Perhaps he is here."

At this, a momentary stirring went about the room, a subtle rustling as when an invisible wind descends, lightly touches the sand, and then is gone.

Until now, I had not observed the man next to me, at my left beside the door. Since I entered the room he sat without motion on the floor, his knees drawn up, his arms resting on them, his face cradled there. Now he abruptly lifted his face and in a single lithe movement stood to his feet. He was the youthful John, the younger son of Zebedee and Salome. My uncle, who admired him greatly, had spoken sometimes of this remarkable young man.

Now John spoke. I have always remembered that as he stood beside me he allowed his right hand to rest lightly on my shoulder. I sat very still. John's voice was strong but not loud, even, and yet there was a suggestion of music in it.

"Fathers and friends," he said, "I am one of the young among you, but I too have thought much of what he did and said when here. I understand it no better than any of you, perhaps not as well as most. My mind reaches for what it cannot grasp, but my heart feels the touch of something it cannot deny."

Having now the attention of all present, John went on, "I think of another aspect of what Jesus said. Yes, he spoke here of his body as broken as bread is broken. Well... I was one who... witnessed the breaking of his body."

Here the voice faltered. All were silent, waiting, wondering. Then, regaining control, John continued: "It seemed so tragic. Why must it be? As I think of the events in this room, now nearly three fortnights ago, a light breaks into my darkness. That night he broke the bread. Why? That he might give it to us. Perhaps he gave his body also to be broken, as was the bread, that somehow, in some deep way, he might give himself to us."

A surge of astonishment swept across the room. But no one spoke, and John went on: "Did not we who followed always feel that he was... well, reaching for us, trying to get through to us? You know how it is when a jar is broken — the contents are released, poured out. Perhaps..."

Here John hesitated, then said tentatively, "Perhaps in the breaking of his body, his spirit was released, poured out, set free, and somehow he is nearer to us now than ever before."

From somewhere one of the men spoke, this voice one I had not heard before: "John, do you not know that philosophers are old men? For one so young, you philosophize too much."

The hand on my shoulder tightened convulsively, then relaxed. After a moment John removed his hand, spread both hands before him in a gesture of patient entreaty, and said: "I am a seeker in quest of a meaning. I must follow the light I see, however dim. I must go where I am led, however strange the place. Are not all amongst us seeing what none have ever seen before? Are not we all together being led where no other has ever been? Already it is on new ground that we walk, and the ground on which we will walk tomorrow is as yet unknown."

John sat again beside me on the flagstones. A ripple of whispers went about the room. The whispers subsided and the stillness returned, but was broken presently by the voice of the woman who had spoken earlier. "Where is he now?" she said. To this there was no response.

"Why are we here?" asked my mother's brother, moving from the philosophical to the practical.

"We are here," replied one of the followers, "because he said that we should wait."

There was then an outbreak of questions:

"Do you think he knows we are here?"

"Did he say we should come to this place?"

"Why did he wish us to remain?"

"What is it that we are waiting for?"

"How long will it be?"

Following this flurry of questions, four or five of the men, closely grouped, spoke together in low tones, and I observed that two or three glanced toward John. Presently one came, bent down before the young apostle, looked searchingly into his face, and then asked, "Did he tell you anything, John?"

"You mean privately?"

"Yes, privately."

"No," replied John, "nothing."

By now, the aura of awe had dissipated somewhat. Thomas, who sat at the table with Simon, now arose, stepped forward a pace, and began to speak: "It is unclear to me whether he actually said we should come to the room, but I feel he meant us to. One thing, though, does I think stand very clearly forth, and I believe it extremely important: he desired that we should remain together."

Thomas paused, then added, "Together. I think he is not through with us yet. Whatever he intends, I feel he wants us together — as though he were with us still."

Appearing to have finished, Thomas ceased speaking. But with no other voice immediately forthcoming, he then resumed: "Since the day Jesus came to some of us when the doors were shut, I have pondered a mystery of him. He once said, 'I go to my Father,' and we believed he spoke of his death. Then he died. But did he go? No. Instead, he came back to us. He must have had a reason. Death ordinarily takes ours away from us. But not him. I feel that he has used death as his means for coming nearer."

Beside me, John gasped as one about to let out a great shout, but nothing came, and every sinew of his body seemed atremble with excitement.

Thomas continued: "What will happen next? Of course I do not know. Our assignment now, as I perceive it, is to be together and to wait."

Appearing again to have finished what he wished to say, Thomas stepped back a pace and bowed slightly.

"We are to wait — forever?" said someone.

"Not forever, no," quickly came a voice. It was the voice of Thaddaeus again, and he continued: "It was only on this very day he told us we should tarry... until —"

"Until when?" asked one.

"Until what?" asked another.

"Who can know?" said someone.

"It is asking what is next upon the earth when men already have seen a fireball split the sky asunder and all mountains have moved to where the seas have been." It was John who said this, inaudibly almost, never lifting his head, as though he was speaking to himself. Being at his side, I heard, and all my lifetime I have marveled at this that he said.

It has been my understanding that, because of previous ties with the Romans, Matthew had not at first stood in good favor with many of the disciples. However, by his loyalty, strength, and good sense, he had by now gained the respect of almost all. I say almost all, for there was a solitary exception, as would become dramatically apparent later.

Matthew was a deliberate man, hesitant somewhat, and slow of speech, methodical. He appeared always to listen well and to speak from having thought. His mind, though not quick, was deep, and although not agile, strong. Now, in a fashion typical of him, he said to all:

"Brothers and sisters, there is much at this time that we do not know. For us, this is a time of searching, for direction, for understanding. Always, in any quest, it is important to ask the right questions. To great degree, we take our directions from the questions we ask, and asking the wrong ones can lead us to the wrong places. The question for us now, it seems to me, is not what may next occur. The question is: What should we now do?"

Here the apostle paused, looking about upon those around

him. Then he continued: "Clearly, we are to await an event sometime forthcoming. Must we know what it is for which we wait? I think not. Let us simply trust. Our need now, I believe, is to be faithful in our waiting and leave the event to God."

"Well spoken, Matthew," said Bartholomew.

By this time, the Eleven, except John, stood as a group near the center of the room. Around the perimeter, two or three deep, the others ranged in broken segments of a circle, some sitting, as was I, on the floor, some on the chairs, and some standing.

One of the disciples spoke to Simon: "Simon, what do you really make of it? The Master walked with us and then he was not; we stood alone on the Bethany Road." There were tears in the voice.

Simon shook his great head and sighed, "I make nothing of it. I do not understand, I just don't know."

At this John arose, and moving to the others clustered there, he said: "Must we know? We know already the super-seding truth: he lives. When one knows the temple stands, is it essential to know in what way every stone was put in place? Is it not of more importance to know the temple's worth, to know the joy and awe of entering there?"

"Must you speak in riddles, John?" asked one.

"It is not that I mean to," he replied. "What I feel and long to say is so much greater than my power of language. Something of the inexpressible wells within me. Don't we all feel it?"

As a stone dropped into water sends out the encircling waves, so did John's comment send a ripple of murmurs about the room.

It was at about this time that James, the Master's cousin, addressed the entire assembly. "Let us give thought," he said, "to this of which Matthew has spoken and likewise John. We are here because the Master bade us tarry. And, as Thomas has said, he has wished us to be together. We are to wait. For what we do not know, and we cannot know for how long. We know not if it will be for moments, days, or years. Necessity requires, I think, that we arrange ourselves for whatever ensuing time may bring. We must give our attention to it, don't you think?"

One of the others then said, "There is much we do not know. Two things, though, I believe we do know: We must remain in this city and we must remain together."

Following this, there was a general hesitation as persons glanced about, one to another, murmuring things but saying little. At length, in small clusters conversations began to take shape, although I heard only a little of all that was said.

After much perplexed discussion, James spoke again: "Let us see if we may sum it up. The Master enjoined us to tarry in Jerusalem, and we have chosen this as our place of gathering. Many of us are from Galilee and some from other places. Jerusalem is a great city, and many disciples and friends are here. If these are willing, as we know already that many are, let us distribute ourselves among them for lodging and food, making this room our constant trysting place for as long as may be. Let it be understood that, except when necessary that any of us be elsewhere, we will, all of us, endeavor to be at this place."

It was so agreed, various area residents offering shelter for the night and certain of the men choosing to remain at the room until dawn. Very quietly then, and very thoughtfully, a major portion of the company moved away, dispersing into the city.

Now the room was in the house of Jotham, the spice and cloth merchant, brother-in-law of Quarantus. Situated on the hilltop in the Upper City not far from the King David Gate, the house was one of the more noble in the area and one of the largest.

Here in this room Gamaliel, a teacher of the law, had

sometimes kept school for his pupils, and here on occasion the owner had stored and showed the merchandise in which he dealt. Sympathetically disposed toward the Master and his followers, he now generously gave consent for this use of the room, even providing such furnishings as were required.

Events of the next days are obscured somewhat in my mind by the passing of much time. I suppose that in some measure they have been displaced by the vast throng of events that have since transpired.

However, mine has been the advantage of being myself a disciple through virtually all my years. All this while, I have lived and moved among others of this Faith, and our frequent gatherings have served me well. Combining our recollections, we have often talked of these events in depth and detail, and so memory has been maintained and from time to time renewed.

Therefore, many things remain clear, standing forth as stars in an unclouded sky.

It is now 53 years after. A long war has ravished the land, Jerusalem lies in ruin, and it is from Pella that I write.

In these years, we of this Faith have stood high on mountain summits and walked sadly in dark valleys. I doubt if ever in history the farthest extremes of joy and sorrow have touched more closely within human spirits than within ours in this time. Great has been the joy to know of wonders this Faith has wrought. But deep has been the sorrow to know what suffering many of our number have been compelled to endure.

What of the tomorrows? We do not know. But this Faith does not rest on knowing. For us of this Faith, the long, long future is sure; only the interval is uncertain. Because of the certainty of that, we can move assuredly through this.

And I think, too, that we may take encouragement from these first disciples who made their way through those first awesome days. They stood beyond the edge of every map. They probed the dimness for any sign of light. They stood midway between two mysteries really: Their recent years with Jesus were as incomprehensible to them as their future was unknown.

Out of their uncertain time, they may speak to us in ours. Their story may help to guide us on our way.

II

It was the third month, the month of Sivan, the end of the latter rain, and the dry time had barely begun. The Feast of Weeks was drawing to its close, and for most people it was a time of much joy. In the countryside the wheat was being garnered, the olives were yellow with bloom, and all things were as green and beautiful as they ever are.

In the city the artisans and the tradesmen went about their affairs in normal ways. That year's Passover disturbances now almost seven weeks past, the city had fairly well settled into its usual routine. Around the temple and about the marketplaces there appeared no evidence of the extraordinary.

In the midst of all this, though, and unknown to most, singular events were transpiring in and around the house of Jotham. On the second day of the ten, going on an errand for someone, as I descended the stair, I came upon two men standing nearby on the street. Both turned to me and one said, "Tell me, son, what is happening here at this place?"

After thinking a little, I replied, "I don't know, sir." Looking at me more closely now and apparently observing my youth, the man offhandedly remarked, "No, you wouldn't, of course," and then shrugged and walked away with the other.

I felt some offense by the man's remark. At that time it was not only I who did not know; no one knew. All were walking where none had ever walked before. None knew what was next or what would be at last.

Time moved at an erratic pace, standing still, it often seemed, then leaping forward in long bounds, impelled by the power of some new occurrence. By day and by night the disciples moved in and out of the room, when present in silence pondering, or in earnest groups conversing, sometimes in a tumult of shouting. There were tensions and tempers, yet often such tenderness as I have never seen since.

When the first night was past and the disciples began to gather in greater numbers from their host homes, the atmosphere was more relaxed than the day before. Simon, the one known as Peter, seemed to have recovered remarkably from the deep sadness that had possessed him.

Speaking as from the crest of a great tide of joy, he addressed the assembled company: "O good and dear friends, how wonderful is this day! Gratitude and gladness well up from deep within me. My heart overflows with thankfulness. I want you to know that you mean more to me than any word of mine can ever tell. You have been good to me, so very good. And our Master, so has he. Whatever future time may bring, I can never cease to love him."

I think Simon may have continued, but a barbed voice stopped him. It was the voice of the other Simon, the Zealot. Sharply, the Zealot interjected, "How long until the cock crows again, Rock?"

A gasp swept across the room like a wave; then stillness fell. Simon made no response. After a moment he turned, moved to the table, sat heavily down, and buried his face in his folded arms. Then his shoulders began shaking with great sobs. Two or three went to him, and others turned to face the Zealot.

One said, "Why?"

With the same edge in his voice as before, the Zealot replied, "You should know why, all of you. Jesus trusted that man's strength so much that he called him a rock, but he proved weak as dust blown by a fickle wind. Behold the weakling now!"

Here the Zealot gestured toward the table where Simon sat weeping. In the Zealot's view, as he saw it then, only weaklings ever cry. Not so, I think, and I think that tears are never more poignant than when a good and brawny man weeps brokenheartedly.

Quickly another of the apostles retorted, answering the Zealot: "I see him, but I think you do not."

"What do you mean?" came the Zealot's sharp reply.

"I mean that you do not really see the man. Do his tears mean nothing to you?"

"Well, he should be crying; he has much to cry about."

At this point another voice broke in. It was the voice of Andrew. Evenly but firmly, Andrew said, "Zealot, I think my brother is not the only man with something to cry about. However, I see no tears coming from you, not yet. Sooner or later, though, will come your time for weeping."

The Zealot made no reply. Instead, he shrugged, threw a contemptuous glance in the direction of the man he had so derisively called "Rock," and turned away, walking outside to the terrace. As several turned to Simon, I moved away to go on a small mission for Joanna.

As for the Zealot's bitter resentment of Simon, this was not quickly to pass. It would continue to prick for many days like a thorn.

As for Simon, later there were smiles relative to his being "Rock" and some of the smiles were his own. So they called him Peter, meaning "rock" of course, and he appeared rather to enjoy it. The name quickly became an informal and cordial appellation by which the man was fondly known. As most will know, during ensuing time, more than 34 years of it, this big-hearted man over and over again proved himself worthy of the name.

Later that day when I returned, having delivered the message Joanna had sent me with, I observed that James, son of Alphaeus, sat pensively alone on the rooftop parapet near the stair. He was a long while there. Then coming into the room, he asked the attention of all present.

As all turned to him he began to speak, his voice atremble. He said, "My brothers, I have been looking deep inside myself, and I see an ugly thing that I had not really seen before. This matter between Simon and the Zealot has spoken to me of a grave fault that is mine. And I cannot bear it."

Clearly in great distress the apostle paused, striving to compose himself. All were intent to hear what James would next say. With strenuous effort and regaining a measure of control, he continued.

"I fear this circumstance of Simon and the cock-crowing has been a vexation for me, as for the Zealot, but in a different way. I was secretly glad when Simon denied his discipleship. I gloated in his failure."

A ripple of movement went about the room, as many disbelievingly turned to others and some dropped their eyes to gaze unseeingly upon the flagstone floor. With strong resolve, the apostle went on.

"Our brother Simon had been, I thought, so sure of himself, so confident, and apparently so much in our Lord's favor. I inwardly exulted when he stumbled. I felt superior and I liked the feeling. I was pleased to see our brother in the pain his blunder caused him. And when he came later, begging our forgiveness, it was with delight that I saw him humbled. Now I have found this ugly thing in me and I am shamed. I know now that I am weaker than he, to rely on the weakness of another man to make me feel strong."

Here James suddenly ceased, turned to Simon, and said pleadingly, "Simon, Simon, can you forgive me, please, please forgive me?"

Simon said not a word, but with the glow of a supreme joy showing through tears so recently shed, he arose, took three firm steps to where James stood, and approaching, threw wide his great arms and brought them together in a mighty embrace about the man's trembling body.

Only then did Simon speak, and I have always remembered the way he precisely accented every word: "My brother, I love you, I love you — and let us ask God to forgive us all." This from Simon — and so soon after all the Zealot had put him through.

By this time there were tears in many eyes and prayers on many lips. After some time of prayer, and as the high emotion of the time subsided somewhat, one of the others asked to speak with the assembly, now numbering about forty. Although I am unable to say with certainty who this was, I well remember the sense of what the man said.

"I wish to confess to all, and to Simon especially, that I have not really forgiven him for deserting our company and denying our Lord. I only made a pretext of doing so; with my lips I did, but not in my heart."

Turning dramatically to Simon, the speaker went on, "Simon, Simon, I do, as of now, forgive you, and I hope you can forgive me."

There was then another embrace from Simon, and there were other embraces and tears of joy here and there about the room.

It was as though the passionate outburst of the Zealot concerning Simon had stirred feelings that had lain a long while latent. As I look back on it now, it seems there were acrid residues that had settled surreptitiously into minds and spirits, and that now a purging time had come.

One caught up in this was Bartholomew, often called Nathanael, a quiet man and well-regarded by all. The happening came as a surprise to everyone. I believe it was sometime during this eventful second day that I observed Bartholomew in earnest conversation with John. After a good while the two walked together to the terrace, where they continued their discussion of what appeared to be some serious issue.

The two at length returning, Bartholomew did a thing that I am sure was very difficult for him to do. Asking the privilege of speaking to the group, he said with some nervousness and much emotion, "I have deeply wronged our brother John. I have told him this. And I feel I must tell all of you. The offense was wholly within me and you would never know. But I know. Without your understanding and your forgiveness, I cannot live with this that I know of me."

Brows furrowed in bewilderment as disciples turned questioningly to one another. But Bartholomew, although gravely distressed, went tenaciously on.

"Some will remember that in this very room Jesus once made it known that one of us would betray him. At that time, many of us speculated in our minds concerning who the betrayer might be. As for me, I suspected John. But worse, I wanted it to be John."

A tide of disbelief went through the company like a shudder. Was this the mild and kind Bartholomew they knew?

He continued: "Deep within my heart, I was host to a giant-size jealousy of John. This young man was always so close to our Lord and I envied this closeness. I think of myself as uncouth and inept; I had not the confidence to draw near, but this young man could and did. I resented his intelligence and vitality. Deep within me there was some ugly thing that wanted him brought down. And I felt that if one so close should prove so false, this would certainly undo him. And I wanted him undone."

None present had ever known this quiet man to speak at such length, nor had any seen him so distraught. All were respectfully attentive as Bartholomew continued.

"It is terrible, this foul thing I have allowed to grow within me. As I have confessed to John, I confess also to all of you. Be merciful to me, if you can."

"We can!" The interruption came from John himself, who stood quietly at Bartholomew's left. "We can and we will," John continued, throwing his right arm around Bartholomew's shoulders.

Turning to the others, he said while gesturing toward Bartholomew: "Here is manhood at manhood's best, don't you think?"

In response, a chorus of affirmation arose throughout the room. John smiled, and Bartholomew brightened a little. Then John said: "It was not required of Bartholomew that he do what he has done. His integrity has spoken from within him. It takes courage to lay bare the heart and it takes trust. And this good man has trusted us, every one of us, to understand. We do, do we not?"

Again a chorus of approval filled the room, and John continued: "Bartholomew would have no dividing barrier to stand in any way between any two of us. He would have nothing impede the growth of community amongst us, nothing either open or secret. He is a strong and brave man. I would be proud if I could call him father."

Here Bartholomew, a man not given to impulse, turned impulsively and swept the young apostle into a close embrace. Then lifting tear-filled eyes, he spoke over John's head, saying just two words: "Thank God!"

A surge of rejoicing was instantly preempted as someone harshly interjected, "Bartholomew, I think you are too generous with the youngster; do you not remember that he and his brother selfishly asked for special privilege in whatever realm the Master might one day rule?"

The room fell suddenly silent, but the silence was quickly broken by a voice from near the doorway. Salome, mother of John and James, had quietly entered and having heard this latest comment, she now spoke: "It was I, not they, who made that request."

All eyes now turned to this small woman, plainly clothed, slightly stooped, with graying hair but a strong and youthful face and perceptive eyes.

"Mother!" cried John as he stepped lightly to her side and took her hand. James smiled but made no move toward her.

Salome was about to continue, but Andrew spoke instead, abruptly, very excitedly, and with uncharacteristic urgency. "I must speak, my friends," he said. "I cannot hear James and John censured for desiring position and privilege without letting you know that I am as much to be censured as they."

Undeterred by the consternation that seized the company, this most modest of apostles plunged relentlessly forward with what he felt compelled to say.

"No, I did not ask to sit at our Lord's right or left, but I had visions of sitting there. I believed I would be rewarded for not asking. I desired my apparent humility to be noted. I was sure that they who sought the top places would never get them; therefore I never asked for one. I felt that my best chance of getting what I wished was to pretend disinterest. And this I did. I used my humility as a ruse to gain the object of my desire. As I look now into my heart this I see, and this I cannot abide."

Andrew paused uncertainly. Then, as though impressed with a sudden thought, he turned abruptly to Simon Peter, who stood close by, and quickly added, "My brother may wish to say something."

Peter did not immediately respond, but appeared preoccupied. All who stood by speculated voicelessly as to what he might say. At last he stepped to Andrew's side, briefly put an arm around him, then withdrew a pace or two, saying: "Andrew, I don't know. Are you seeing yourself as you are or are you drawn too much into the current of confession that seems just now to run so strong amongst us? By too much looking within, we may sometimes see ghostly specters that are not really there.

"On the other hand, perhaps you were indeed a selfish seeker for place and privilege, and perhaps so was I. If so, my method was other than yours. I spoke openly and often, always with high praise and confidence. Was I false? I don't really know. I did not believe so, nor do I now. But I know this: I always, always loved and adored our Lord; I still do, and by all that is within me, I always will. Yes, I failed him, many times maybe, but one time notably. I lost my courage but never my love. And my prayer now is that my courage may survive equally with my love and that both will be forever strong."

"May I please say something now?" It was Salome again and as she spoke she beckoned to James that he come and join John and her. This James did and the brothers' mother went on to say: "I think you know that Jesus was my sister's son. I had known him from childhood, and I had always believed he would grow up to be someone great. In these last two years or so, along with you, I believed him destined to be a king, liberating Israel, and wisely ruling a free and peaceful land. I was proud of these two sons of mine and so very pleased they were faithful and loyal to their cousin. Knowing Jesus as I did, and knowing my sons as I do, I thought it right they should rule with him in his kingdom."

Some assuming Salome spoke in defense of herself and her sons, a surge of apprehension suddenly welled within the room. This rapidly faded, however, as she went on: "How blind I was and slow of understanding. I knew not what I asked, for I did not know the meaning of Jesus when he spoke of his kingdom. I do not know the meaning yet. I suppose, though, that all now know what his kingdom is not: It is not Israel or Judea. From the moment I heard the response of Jesus to my request, I have known that the kingdom of which he spoke is a kingdom unlike any ever before seen on earth."

Here with great excitement John spoke, whether interrupting his mother I do not know, for I have never known if she intended to go on saying other things.

John fairly shouted, "Oh, my mother, bless you, and God be praised! You have said more than any of us yet know. Oh, my dear ones of this discipleship, our dream of kingdom is not dead! It did not perish at Golgotha. Behold the light on yon horizon: it is not the sunset; it is the rising! With all my heart, with all my mind, I believe it true: Though crucified, our Lord is yet a king, and his kingdom somewhere waits. One day we shall understand, and we shall find it at last."

Among the company there were those who smiled and shook their heads in wise ways, as if to say, "Well, here goes John, being mysterious again," but all such feelings were left unsaid.

After all that had transpired in the room following the Zealot's stunning outburst, the company appeared mentally and emotionally fatigued. It had been a drama of the unexpected and exhaustive of mind and spirit.

As I look upon it now, though, I believe that on this day two major movements were beginning to take shape. The one was a refinement of spirit and attitude among the disciples, making way for community at last. The other was a quest for understanding, a struggle to comprehend the meaning of the incredible leader these people had followed so long.

As the day drew near its close, one of the disciples summed it up as well as any might: "We wait, not knowing for what, but we may be near understanding why."

"Your meaning?" asked another.

The first replied, "Perhaps we must wait because we are not yet prepared for whatever is before us."

A third voice now came into the conversation. It was the voice of Joseph Barsabas, saying, "I did not know Jesus as long as some of you, nor as well as many. But I knew him as the most purposeful of persons. I suspect he never did anything except when there was purpose in it. And without doubt, when he instructed us to remain in Jerusalem he had good reason for it. I strive to recall all he said yesterday on the Bethany road."

About thirty heard him. These now thoughtfully compared memories of their final walk with him. There was no doubt of it: He had enjoined them to tarry in Jerusalem. But why? Had he given them any sign of what they should expect? Only that they should await a promise of God, only that they would receive a power. But what of the meaning here? What should they look for, strive for, anticipate?

To keep a tryst with a stranger, there must be a sign by which to know him. But for these disciples there was no sign. When going forward to whatever place is next, some travel instruction is normally needed. But these disciples had none; the Master's only word was "wait."

Waiting meant trusting; perhaps it always does. Once they had followed when Jesus beckoned; now they needed to trust when they could no longer see his hand or hear his voice. They must hold it firmly true that he had not abandoned them. They had an appointment with the unknown, and they knew neither with what nor for when.

Here they were, of necessity, in Jerusalem, and of necessity together. There, everywhere beyond the walls of Jotham's house, scattered throughout the city, were hostile Romans and hostile Jews, those who had crucified the Lord. How did these view his followers now? Were other crucifixions in the offing? None could surely know. They knew only that they must remain together and that they must wait.

III

As I remember, the third day dawned bright and beautiful. Most nights I slept at our home, not far removed from the house of Jotham. This night, however, I had remained at the room, sleeping on a pallet alongside four or five of the men who had chosen also to remain. I think that in the whole of the ten days, either by day or night, the room was never without persons in or about it. There appeared to be the feeling that the place must be constantly attended. I think that the matter was never discussed, that there was rather a kind of subconscious agreement that perpetual vigil must be kept. Why, I have never fully understood.

On this day, disciples began gathering with the coming of dawn, among them Mary and Joanna, two women from the Galilean village of Magdala. Mary was deeply devoted to Jesus and had lately proven herself one of the most faithful of his followers.

Mary's earlier life at Magdala had been an ordeal of circumstance. Without father or mother from age eight, her life for a long while was largely that of a beggar on the streets. As she grew older, a few offered friendship, but not most, and among these she was shunned as inferior and unwelcome. On occasion kind persons placed gifts in her hand, but most men were more likely to toss coins on the ground for the sport of seeing her grovel for them. And there were men seeing her otherwise who ogled like predators stalking their prey. She fought hard to maintain her womanhood, sometimes winning, and apparently sometimes losing. As she would later say, it was as though angels and demons were at war within her.

At the depth of her misery Mary had met Jesus, and by

this meeting her life had been transformed. As one dug from a deep pit relishes light and air, so was her feeling for life and for him.

Joanna, by her intelligence, poise, and good manner, had become chief stewardess in the household of Herod Antipas, governor of Galilee and Perea. Earlier she became a disciple of Jesus, traveling with the company as her duties allowed. Through her influence, the governor came to have a sincere interest in Jesus, desiring to meet him, as at length he did.

Upon the transformation of Mary, Joanna welcomed her warmly into the company of disciples, and the two were ever after closely intertwined in friendship. Although the roads of life the two had thus far traveled could scarcely have been more divergent, the two now shared a common devotion, and it was this more than anything else that drew them together and held them close.

Upon her arrival on this day, Joanna called me aside and bade me carry a message to another, one lodging at the house of Mary, the Mary of Jerusalem, the mother of John Mark. Arriving at the house and calling for one named Ashabel, I was shown into the presence of a most beautiful woman. Hers was not merely a beauty of form; hers was also, and chiefly, a beauty of depth. In the noontime of her life, she appeared frail yet supremely strong.

During the days following, I learned more and more of this amazing woman. She was also from Magdala, an acquaintance of both Mary and Joanna. Hers was a finely tuned and highly sensitized spirit, and hers the noblest of all aspirations: To live in the full dimension of all that life is and to become all she could possibly be.

Her husband and her only child having lately died, she suffered greatly the pain of loss. When tragedy had befallen, one of the foremost to offer comfort had been Mary, only a short while before rescued by Jesus from the streets of Magdala.

Amazed and inspired by the transformation wrought in Mary, Ashabel had gently inquired in what way the change came about. "It was Jesus of Nazareth," Mary had replied. "It was by him that my life was restored to me." From that moment, Ashabel had sought to find Jesus.

Learning at length that Jesus and the company were in Jerusalem for Passover, she had joined a small caravan going there. As the travelers had passed the Damascus Gate, entering the city, they had been halted by a great mass of people and a strange procession moving toward Mount Golgotha. Arriving thus on the day Jesus died, Ashabel had never met him at all.

She later said she saw above the seething mass only the huge wooden cross that Jesus carried. I suspect that in this moment her agony was almost as great as his. She resolved, however, to tarry a while in Jerusalem and learn of Jesus whatever was possible.

Having delivered Joanna's message, I returned to the room. An hour later Ashabel came up the stair and was greeted there by Joanna and Mary. After embraces, these three women of Magdala walked together into the room. Although it was in an unobtrusive manner that they entered, most eyes somehow turned to them as they passed the threshold.

Joanna spoke: "Mary and I have with us a friend from Magdala. Her name is Ashabel. She has come seeking Jesus."

Among the disciples, Joanna was well-known, respected, and much-loved. Now, as she finished speaking, an uneasy silence fell across the assembly, most persons groping for some proper thing to say. The awkward quiet was broken only when one turned to another, saying, "I fear she has come too late." Although spoken only a little above a whisper, the words cut into the silence virtually as would a shout.

For what seemed an interminable time all was quiet again, as no one could think of what ought to be said. Eventually, though, came this response: "How can we be sure of that?" The speaker was John.

During these awkward moments the three women had continued to stand together uncertainly near the doorway. Presently John's older brother graciously moved toward them, saying, "Come, come to the table and sit; take some cakes and milk and let us talk."

As the three women and several others of the company moved to the chairs, others present resumed their various pursuits. At the table a long and intricate conversation followed. So singular was it that the attention of those standing about was drawn to the seven or eight at the table, until soon a rather large audience stood listening.

I shall not undertake to speak in detail of all that was said, only to give the general sense of it. I think that much said here had never before been said or thought in the whole history of the world.

The conversation began as Matthew spoke to Ashabel: "So you seek Jesus?"

"Yes," Ashabel answered simply.

"Why?" asked Matthew.

Ashabel then, with a little aid here and there from Joanna and Mary, told the story of her sorrow and of a longing of spirit she deeply felt. But why should it be Jesus whom she would seek? Why not some other? Because of Mary, Ashabel said, because Mary had spoken as she had of Jesus and because of the transformation that was apparent in this woman's life. Ashabel spoke movingly of the wave of hopelessness that overtook her upon discovering in Jerusalem that Jesus was even then being taken away for crucifixion.

At the table John sat somewhat apart, intently listening, but speaking not at all for a long while. At length, though, he quietly and very gently addressed the woman from Magdala: "Ashabel, it may be that your coming is not too late."

All eyes turned questioningly to John. "How can you say

this, John?" asked one of the men.

"I am not sure I really know," the young apostle replied, "but, with Thomas, I strongly believe that Jesus is not through with us yet."

"Are you saying," asked one, "that Jesus will come to us again?"

It was with extreme care that John responded: "I do not know if he will or if he will not. But I think it does not greatly matter."

Hearing this, the assembled group reacted with a start. It does not matter? Why, John? How could anything matter more?

Quietly and thoughtfully, John made response to the many questions: "There is much I do not know, but this I do: He lives! I need not see him cross this threshold to know that he is here."

Gasps of astonishment were audible. But John continued, as calmly and deliberately as before: "He made his exit at the same gate we all do, the gate of death, but as none before have ever done, he came back. And mark you, it was to us he came. He came to us who had seen and heard and followed. Why so? Perhaps to let us know that, although he died, death had not taken him away."

A sense of awe had been increasingly apparent in John's voice as he spoke, and as he now paused, that same sense seemed to permeate the room. There was utter stillness. How very odd it is that the small things are sometimes most remembered, and so it is as I recall those moments now: I remember most the sound of my own breathing.

It was a long while before anyone spoke, and then it was John again, continuing with the thread of his thought: "If our Master has taught us anything, he has taught us this: We live in more than body. And I think so does he. Yes, of course we live in association with these bodies we call ours, but it seems that he is able to disassociate from his. He is now free of it. Death has severed that connection. It may be that the ultimate goal of life is freedom; and if this be so, then death has served him well. Oh, my dear fathers and mothers among you, pray forgive the vision of a youth, but I need not look upon his face or touch his hand to know that Jesus lives. As for finding him, I deeply feel that the time will never be too late."

Again a deep stillness settled as all present grappled with strange new thoughts that battered and strained the mind.

As I recall, it was Thomas who next spoke. Giving rapt attention to all that had transpired, this cautious and careful disciple had stood quietly alongside the great table. Now, arms folded across his chest, he lowered his face, closed his eyes, and spoke reflectively as though speaking to himself.

"There was a time," said Thomas, "when I would not believe him living except as I see and touch him. This I once did and I need not do so again. It is my guess that for the sake of people like me and to lead us gently on into faith, he once or twice used his freedom to assume again the body that was broken so that we might touch and see. And I would guess, too, that as he offered to me his wounded side and hands, he felt again all the pain of piercing spear and driven nails. I rejoice that he can now be free of that. Though earth tremble and stars fall, I shall yet believe he lives, and I do not any longer require the confirmation of sight or touch."

Here Thomas lifted his eyes, looking upward as into a far distance, and with an imploring gesture of his hands spoke more loudly than before, and somewhat nostalgically: "Oh yes, I wish I could see him, of course I do. But even as one blind may be sure of a sunrise, I can accept without seeing. I do not require the evidence of a body to prove that spirit and person are real."

Here the apostle lowered his gaze, glanced to those around him, and added an apparent afterthought. "For that matter," he said, "all the bodies in the world could never stand as proof of spirit. This is truth that must be found some other way and each must find it for himself."

With this Thomas paused, smiled, and then added, "It cannot be passed one to another like biscuits at the dinner table."

Even-tempered and genteel, Thomas was known throughout the company as one of careful thought and well-considered judgments, a man who learned willingly yet held opinions firmly. He was generally heard with respect and so was it now. Several nearby turned to embrace the man, the first being John.

As for John, the young apostle's perceptivity, depth of mind, and remarkable gift of speech had by this time virtually overcome the handicap of his youth. While not heard with a respect equal to that generally accorded Thomas or James, he was heard with a fascination even greater than that enjoyed by them. At first John had been tolerated much as adults in serious enclave might tolerate an adolescent child, but these adults had soon discovered the child in many ways more mature than they.

Trying to fathom the mysteries of the Master, there were those present who sometimes expressed bewilderment and some doubt. On this day, however, as conversations continued around the table and about the room, it was uniformly felt that in some way Jesus was not gone as others of the dead are gone. There appeared to be no question about that.

But now another question arose. In earlier days, many had witnessed wonders wrought by Jesus and lives remarkably transformed as Mary's had been. But might such wonders and transformations be expected still? The question was this: May he yet do for Ashabel what he had done for Mary? Much discussion followed.

It was Stephen, Jerusalem's beloved coppersmith, who skillfully drew attention to the critical issue. It came about in this way: After some talk of remarkable things Jesus had been seen to do, Stephen quietly asked, "And how much of this did he need his body for?"

The question dropped like a large stone into a small pool; it made a monstrous impression. To what extent was it by physical presence and power that Jesus did what he did? And to what extent was it by a power of some other kind?

Simon Peter spoke: "The mother of my wife lay ill at our house. Jesus came and took her hand and she was instantly whole again. Was that done by the power of a hand? Was it a physical force that made the woman well? I think not, for all the physical force exerted there would not have lit even a single small candle."

Another spoke: "Some of us will remember that Jesus was nowhere near the place or the man when he brought healing to a city officer at Capernaum."

Rising from her place at the table, her voice both subdued in awe and vibrant with excitement, Mary said, "And I am Mary of Magdala, up from the streets and the shame, and he never even touched me!"

Now, as Joanna and Ashabel also arose, Ashabel said, "It gives me hope. Perhaps the time is not too late. Perhaps I shall find him yet."

"God be praised!" exclaimed one, Prochorus, as I remember.

The three women of Magdala moved to the doorway, crossed the terrace, and were about to descend the stair. Simon Peter restrained them, saying kindly, "Ashabel, you bless us by your coming. You bless us in a way you do not know. By your search for him we have long followed, you compel our attention to matters that demand deep thought. And this is good."

Smiling, Ashabel replied, repeating the thing she had earlier said: "Perhaps it is not too late; perhaps I shall find him yet." So saying, she turned and descended the stair with Mary and Joanna.

In the room and about the terrace everyone seemed to know that something had happened, but no one seemed to know precisely what. By the questing of Ashabel, the disciples had been forced into unexplored regions of thought; now, by the event next forthcoming, they would be forced even farther.

Day by day the Zealot was often absent a great deal from the room, and so it had been on this day. Having entered during the previous conversation, he had stood nervously near the door, furtively observing all that went on about him. Two or three times he had moved forward a pace or so, appearing about to speak. But he had not spoken.

The three women now gone, the Zealot restlessly made one or two revolutions around the room and then stopped near the center of it. Turning to the apostles and disciples clustered about the table there, his burning eyes blazing even more intensely than usual, he fairly shouted: "You say he lives! At least, some of you say that. How can you? The tyranny of Rome lays waste to our land. Our people suffer. Injustice and oppression abound. If he lives, tell me, how is it then he does not act? You say he has power; how is it then he does not use this power he has? You seem to say, some of you, that he can yet do things. Then why is it that he does nothing about the cruelty of those who oppress us? Tell me. I need to know. I must know."

When speaking passionately, as he was wont to do, the Zealot had a way of punctuating his words with a gesture that was uniquely his own. His left arm, elbow to fingertips, was as a hammer pummeling the air with sharp upward strokes. Hand closed, but with forefinger extended upward, the piercing jabs were delivered in perfect synchronization with his speech, word by word.

Now, as that expressive left hand dropped to his side, the Zealot flashed a defiant look about the room, his breast heaving from want of breath and from emotional agitation.

Although he waited for someone to speak, no one did.

Moments passed. Then the Zealot spoke again: "Why is it no one answers me? Have you no answer? Is there none? I want our people to be free again. I want the stolen kingdom restored to Israel. I had trusted that Jesus would be the one to do this. I gave my life to him for the sake of this hope. But he died. They killed him. And he is only the first. Mark me well, others will also die. As long as Romans rule, blood will overflow the nations, and most of it will not be Roman blood. You may not feel the tremors that shake the world. But I feel them. As for our people, our greatest need is to be freed from the Roman yoke. Perhaps only God can do it. But if God does not, then many of us will die trying."

Again, exhausted by the vigor of his speech, the Zealot paused, and again the left arm fell to his side. Again, no one spoke. Then, after waiting a little, the Zealot spoke again, now in a lower tone and slowly, the arm limp at his side. He said, "I am tired, so very tired. I do not understand. I want to love him; I want to believe in him. But how can I? I am lost; I have been lost since the day Jesus died. Until then I had my hope to guide me. But hope died when he did. And I am lonely now. Bereft of hope, I am sick of heart and lonely."

If tears may flow in voices, there were tears in the voice of the Zealot as he spoke, and this despite his feeling that only weak men ever cry.

With a deep sigh, the man quietly said, "Forgive me, friends," and turned and strode toward the door, four or five following. On the terrace, they restrained him momentarily, two or three clasping his hand or embracing him. Then alone, a pathetic figure, the Zealot was gone, descending the stair.

In the room, it was as though the sun had gone down and dark clouds obliterated the moon and all stars. Many new emotions had been generated by the Zealot in these last moments.

The man impulsively revealed more of himself than most had ever seen. Always before he had appeared assertive, strong, and confident. What most, though, had long known was now clearly affirmed: The troubled apostle was a man of utter sincerity, sometimes misguided or mistaken perhaps, but totally committed to the ideals he held and wholly unselfish.

But now an enormous vulnerability had made itself known. Visionary and dreamer, he had seen his visions and dreams die when Jesus died, and the hopes that had been three years building within him had now come crashing down. The frustration and disappointment were tearing at his soul, and he had found no way to reckon with them. Which direction he would turn, what he would now do, stood in all minds as a critical unknown. I believe that among the disciples at this time the most troubling anxiety concerned the Zealot and his state of mind and spirit.

But there was also this troubling question the man had raised: If the Risen and Living One willed well for Israel and for justice, then what about Rome? The answer, if there was an answer, was due him. Inevitably, the company fell into conversation about it.

One observed: "Most of us have questions of our own; I wonder therefore if we are competent to answer his."

"But we must try," said another.

My uncle sent me with a message for my mother, and so I was not witness to all that followed. Later, though, I learned of it from others and now have, I think, a general knowledge of what was done and said. It was somewhat in this way that the discussion developed: If Jesus, living still, might be expected still to act, what sort of action might be expected of him? Would he call angels to deal with Roman legions? Would it be his purpose to destroy men who wore the uniform and carried the weapons of Rome? If he were to intervene in human conflict, would he choose among adversaries, destroying one that another may survive? Would his chief concern be for the welfare of nations or of people, for issues or for persons?

Yes, the reasoning continued, it is evil this thing the Romans are doing, and in this conflict reason is on Israel's side. In what way had Jesus always dealt with persons who were evil or involved with evil doings? No one could remember a time when he had clobbered them. Yes, he had spoken harshly of them but never had he injured them. Yes, it was generally agreed, if Jesus were to enter the conflict, his way of doing so would not be any of the usual ways.

Further, not only would he work in his own way, but also in his own time. Who may know, therefore, but that he is working already? The thought of this struck many with great force.

I was told that at one juncture in the discussion John spoke of having witnessed the crucifixion of Jesus. He said that the Roman soldier in charge, deeply moved, proclaimed at last that Jesus was truly one come from God.

Then John had said, "If such change might occur in every Roman, what then would Rome become? Perhaps Jesus would make peace among men by working such transformation in the attitude of every man, Roman and Jew, everywhere and always."

I shall never forget the instance of my return from my mother's house. My Uncle Thaddaeus met me on the terrace, inquiring into a matter concerning her. As we talked, we observed the Zealot come up the stair, with him a man who was stranger to us. Bartholomew, who stood nearby, whispered to my uncle, "Who is that man?" My uncle made no reply but looked directly toward Bartholomew and shook his head, as though saying "I do not know."

As the two men approached, it was apparent that the Zealot had recovered somewhat from the trauma of hours earlier. He said, "This is my friend Zebulon Brashabe. We met in the market some weeks ago."

The newcomer was short of stature and much heavier than would be normal for his height. His round face was sallow, his eyes rather bulged, and his long black hair, oiled down slick against his skull, was bound tightly by a band at the back of his neck. Finely clothed and well perfumed, his was the persona of one of great importance.

Early in the conversation, it developed that the man was from Capernaum, a steward in the synagogue there, a dealer in pottery, perfume, and incense. He had been many days in Jerusalem, awaiting the arrival of a caravan of Nabatean traders coming in from Petra. At the chance meeting with the Zealot he had made some disparaging comment about the Romans, and the Zealot had from that moment felt he had found a true and like-minded friend. Since then the two had been often together, the man from Capernaum appearing always sympathetic with the concerns the Zealot so deeply felt and so freely expressed. Further, he had insinuated to the Zealot that he possessed privileged information concerning Jesus, and the Zealot had believed him.

The man's ability to dominate in this relationship with the troubled apostle served to heighten his already towering sense of importance. Of this the Zealot was unaware, possessed as he was by his passion for Israel's liberation. Rather, he seemed to draw great comfort from what he believed to be the newcomer's warm friendship.

During the brief time the Zealot and Zebulon Brashabe were present at the room there were several who wished to speak seriously and kindly with their troubled fellow, but there was no chance of that, not ever. The Capernaumite managed always to keep himself at the center of everything. Although his leaving took the Zealot also away, all present were relieved to see him go.

Later the man would return, however, and with his returning inflict a wound that pains yet and may never heal.

IV

Soon after dawn the following day, John made it known to all that the mother of Jesus would visit the room sometime before the day's end.

Since Passover, Mary had remained in Jerusalem, a guest in the home of Joseph of Arimathea and his wife Marshia. It was Marshia who had first drawn the attention of her husband to Jesus, and it was largely through her influence that this important citizen had given Jesus and the disciples aid and support in many ways.

In response to the invitation of Joseph and Marshia, and at the insistence of John, Mary had become resident in their home, awaiting, as were all others, whatever might next occur. She was caught in a profound emotional quandary between grief for the crucifixion of her only son and astonishment at all that had happened since.

Mary's husband, a widower at the time, had brought five children to their marriage and these she had loved and cared for as her own. The kind and gentle Joseph of Nazareth, now seven years dead, and his children now mostly indifferent to her son and to her, Mary bore a heavy burden of sorrow.

Lately, however, her burden had been relieved a little. Having given only scant attention to Jesus, Joseph's youngest son, James, who was in Jerusalem for Passover, had been deeply moved by events involving him. It was as a man transformed that James returned to Nazareth, and it was now Mary's hope that there he might influence other members of the family. This transformation of James had come as the first rift in a solid phalanx of hostility and as welcome as a live spark found amid the ashes of a dying fire on a cold winter night.

There was, in and around Nazareth, a cadre of resentful

men who for more than two years had conspired to discredit Jesus, and some among Mary's own neighbors and family had come under the influence of it. So effective was this effort that down to our own time, now 53 years later, there is as yet no community of disciples either at Nazareth or in the immediate area. While communities have been formed virtually everywhere, there are none here.

Although Jesus had grown to manhood in Nazareth, and the village had been Mary's home through most of her lifetime, she was not ever to return. For her, the savage animosity of many in this area was ever a grief lying heavily upon her until the very day of her death, now more than twenty years ago.

On this day following John's announcement of Mary's expected arrival, there was upon most a mood of excited anticipation. As the hours went by, most eyes turned more than usual to the stair.

But it was the Zealot who first came. Heavily ascending tread by tread and approaching a number who stood on the terrace, he was clearly in a state of much distress. These and others greeted him gladly, offering comments they hoped would be helpful. As conversation developed, and as the man softened in response to friendship, the distraught disciple spoke anxiously of the circumstance that now distressed him most.

He had encountered a disturbing disillusionment. As is common with disillusionments, this one centered on a person, a Jerusalem citizen named Banis Barodis. The man was a money lender and investor who had grown rich through shrewd operations and at high cost to many people.

From more than a year earlier, this Barodis had represented himself to the Zealot and to a few others as a staunch champion of Israel's cause against the Romans, leading these lovers of freedom to believe he stood ready to finance a major movement against Rome. As possible, the Zealot and

47

these few others had worked together with him on a scheme to provide enormous aid at whatever time Jesus would at last decide to challenge the Romans, as all believed he would.

In these last days since the crucifixion of Jesus, the Zealot had sought to pursue with this man the initiatives earlier conceived. The Zealot, however, had been appalled to discover that Banis Barodis had lost all interest. At last, only the evening before, the whole truth had come out, and the truth was this: From the beginning, Banis Barodis had involved himself in the freedom movement because he had seen in this a chance to add enormously to his wealth and power. If a successful revolt could be instigated, he would then be in position to take the best skimmings from every pot. His interest, his only interest, had been the economic advantage to himself of any kingdom Jesus might establish and rule.

Now at last Barodis had said to the Zealot, "You stupid fool, let me lay this out where even you can see it. First of all, you should have known my purpose from the start. But your naive altruism blinded you to that. Now that your leader is dead, you should know that I have no further interest in you or these freedom sentiments of yours. My only interest is to stand well with whoever has the power. If your Jesus might have had it, I would have lined up with him. But since Rome has it, I'll be nobly Roman. These people you prattle about — I care nothing for them; they are not worth my caring. You may go ahead and love them if you choose; I will love only me. Stupid fool, now you know. Do not pester me again."

Thus the Zealot had discovered the selfish and evil intent of this most hypocritical of men. And so the wounded apostle's bruised and battered dream had suffered yet another blow. But a heavier blow was yet to fall and immediately would.

There was a flurry of attention as movement was seen on the stair. The person coming, though, was not Mary but was instead the fragrant fat man from Capernaum. Observing closely, I think one might have detected a malevolent glint in his bulging eyes.

Within moments, the man had made himself the center of attention and was smoothly in control of the conversation. By comments he made and questions he asked, it was soon apparent that it was his objective to probe matters concerning Jesus. Having at length manipulated his audience into the position he desired, his voice dripping with all the nectar of the deceitful, he launched into a rather formal address: "I do believe your beloved Teacher was born before his mother was married. This is what I hear. Perhaps you do not really know. Perhaps I should not have mentioned it.

"There may be, though, for that matter, a great deal that you do not know. Indeed, for your comfort it is probably best that you not know. Oh, I am sorry; I seem to be saying all the wrong things."

The man feigned great embarrassment. But he continued, his tone apologetic, as though in explanation of himself: "I suppose the difficulty is that people confide in me; all know me as a man of honor; they know I will keep their confidences. You understand, a man must be strong to hold important knowledge and not impart it. And I shall not, ever."

As the speaker paused, all stood about him in dazed perplexity. For moments he stood before them as one congratulating himself. Then he continued: "One must think of others. Should I disclose all I know of this young man's birth and of his mother, many would be injured, and I would be the very last to wish harm for anyone. As for the man Joseph, being dead, he can no longer speak for himself, and so I cannot bear to speak of him.

"And then, of course, it is usually better that the dark side of things be left in the dark; they appear only uglier in the light. And it may be better that good people such as yourselves should live by an illusion rather than face unpleasant truth. Not for a moment or in any way would I want to disturb the peace of your mind or spirit."

Obviously wholly pleased with his performance, the speaker again paused, but now there was an interruption. Simon Peter moved forward and faced the man, towering chest and shoulders above him. Before the Capernaumite could resume the weaving of his sinister web, Peter spoke in the full strength of his voice, "Why, sir, do you tell us this?"

Blinking two or three times and swallowing once, the speaker responded, again in a tone of the apologetic: "Oh, of course, I tell you this because I seek to be your friend, and friends stand always ready to help one another. In friendship and in the interest of what is of most help for you, I merely warn you to be alert and watchful.

"No, no. I cannot bring myself to the point of telling you all I know, but I should be remiss did I not advise you that things are not always as they appear. On occasion, there are dark secrets that may lie a long while hidden. But they will come out.

"It is a painful thing I do in warning you as I am, but a man must think of his fellows and a man must keep his honor sacred. Although it sometimes requires him to do the painful thing, he must maintain his character in impunity and carefully guard his integrity. Why do I tell you this? Because I, Zebulon Brashabe, am a man of honor."

The cleverly crafted address now completed, the company stood about in silent astonishment.

During the performance, I had especially observed the Zealot. Terribly distraught, pale and trembling, he had near the end of it turned unsteadily to the table, fallen dejectedly onto a chair, and buried his face in his folded arms. In this one day, the troubled apostle had now encountered his second disillusionment; another whom he had considered friend and colleague was proven false.

Of this all were aware except Brashabe himself. He appeared still to be pleased with his performance and clearly awaited whatever response might come from the assembled disciples. He had, without doubt, anticipated consternation and grave distress. He obviously assumed that his speech would create alarm, perhaps panic. He apparently visualized a general confusion, a scene of panic over which he could wield control and continue to fan the flame he had so cleverly lit.

The man waited for reaction, but there was none. About him, no one moved and no one spoke. On every side, from expressionless faces, all eyes were fixed firmly upon his. He glanced about in all directions and then again more anxiously now. Then his smirk faded and his face overclouded with bewilderment.

After minutes, he finally barked, "Well, say something, some of you!" But no one did; nowhere did a facial expression change and all eyes continued to bore in upon him. Those eyes spoke no anger or hostility, only pity, a language that even Brashabe eventually began to understand. And it was too much for him. Nowhere in the depths of his deceitful soul could he find a means for dealing with it. At length, defeated, the aromatic little fat man from Capernaum turned and stalked away.

So far as I know, none of our people ever saw Zebulon Brashabe again. But over a period of three or four years, we sometimes heard news of him. Apparently, he went about throughout the northern precincts claiming knowledge of evil in connection with the birth and life of Jesus. A foremost conspirator in the West Gennesaret cadre of the Lord's enemies, he apparently never gave up his campaign of defamation until he was at last silenced by death.

In his hurried exit Zebulon Brashabe had barely cleared the stair when three women appeared and ascended it. They were Marshia, wife of Arimathea; Mary, the mother of Jesus;

and Salome, sister of Mary and mother of James and John. Warmly greeted by the two sons of Salome and then by many others, the three made their way into the room. There was great excitement that Mary had come.

As conversation developed, John said to all, "If any man may have two mothers, that man is I, one who bore me and one who was given me. I am, of all men, most blessed." With this, John put out his arms, embraced both, and drew them to him.

After a moment, the young apostle turned to Mary, saying, "I believe, beloved one, that I now speak for all gathered here. We are all together earnestly involved in an effort to understand your son, to know with certainty the meaning of him. It is usual that mothers know more of their children than any other may know. Have you anything you can tell us about Jesus?"

Mary silently stepped to the table with the other women following. She lightly laid a hand on a shoulder of the Zealot as she passed, and then she and the others found chairs and seated themselves. With all chairs filled and others of the company gathered about, the mother of Jesus began to speak.

I think that all present would hold this time in memory as long as mind would endure. In only a few moments, this modest small woman gave expression to thoughts of towering importance. Over the ensuing years, her utterances have been reviewed and pondered both in private conversation and large assembly.

It is from the sum of all this that I undertake now to give the sense of what she said. It was with voice subdued and reflective that Mary spoke, her words so softly spoken as to be at times inaudible almost: "I think it all began one marvelous day in spring. I sat alone at a great oak on a hilltop not far from our village. From behind me the setting sun cast a celestial glow against the entire sky. The hills and valleys were tinted with it, and of it creating their own designs of light and shadow. All around and over all, the earth was washed with a brush I think only God knows how to use. I was at peace.

"There came a gentle wind, moving not across as winds mostly do, but it seemed to encircle me. Like a caress, I felt it touching. And there was the light that seemed to float in from all sides and converge and gather around me there.

"Mine was an ecstasy such as I had never known before, nor have I since. I lay back on the grass, closed my eyes, and let my spirit soar. Then I slept. I dreamed, and the dream was two dreams in one. There was the remembered dream, and as for the other, when I awakened the dream was gone. Of my unremembered dream I know only this: it was beautiful. Whatever the place, it was lovely there; whatever happened, it was good.

"Never have I understood it, but from that day I have ever felt a high destiny pulling at my soul. And since that day other mysteries have followed that one.

"It was later, early in winter, that my son was born. From the start, and for my sake I think, Joseph loved him as did I. Into his big and generous heart he took both my son and me. Oh how good and patient and kind was Joseph! He was much older than I, but how utterly devoted to me. But seven years ago I saw my husband die, and now seven weeks ago my son.

"We mothers bear our sons only to lose them, do we not? We give ourselves to them only to see them give themselves to others. Worthily or unworthily, they do. We love them only to surrender them at length to other loves.

"I am, though, of all mothers most blessed. This son of mine gave himself to the most worthy of loves. I think he loved, truly loved, the world, the whole of it. And if he lives, still he loves. And I believe he lives.

"I can think of no greater love I may give him than that to which he gave himself. I never understood him; he was always somewhere beyond me, but I always believed in him.

"I do not know how the hardened hearts of men may be softened and made tender again, but I think he knows. If any love can ever move the world, it is his that can. If any love may stir dead souls to life, I think that his is that love. I dare yet to hope that I have not loved in vain; I believe that yet somehow he will bless the world as no other ever has and perhaps as no other ever can.

"How this may come about I do not know. To find this out, my dear ones, this is the task that is for you."

Here Mary quickly arose, lifted her voice slightly, and repeated, "This, my dear ones, is the task that is for you."

Then, continuing to stand, she spoke very softly again: "What has he done by dying? This is the question that besets me most. I knew him well enough to know this: They did not take my son's life; he gave it. I think there was purpose in his doing that.

"It falls to you and to all who search for understanding to discover what his purpose is, and then to do all that may be done to see that purpose realized. You who have been his disciples, I think your discipleship is but begun. You who have followed thus far, follow on.

"I pray God will bless and guide you on your way, wherever it may lead. It is with deep love that my sisters and I leave you now."

Within moments this remarkable woman was gone. Apostles and disciples stood silently and saw her go. And all knew that their role in this great drama was greater than they had yet dreamed.

An episode immediately forthcoming that would affirm the truth of this came from an unexpected source and in a strange way.

As a great relief to all, during these days the gatherings at the room had been wholly ignored by both Roman and Jewish authorities. They appeared to feel that the crucifixion had settled whatever issues there were. They seemed eager to be done with the whole matter and to avoid any further thought of it.

From time to time elsewhere in the city, uniformed Romans were seen usually in groups of two or three, but none came near the room.

However, a tall stranger of mature years, obviously Roman and always alone, had been often seen lingering about. Straightaway after the visit of Mary, Salome, and Marshia, the tall stranger approached me on the street, saying, "I have often seen you coming and going as a messenger might. May I please ask that you carry a message for me? It is important to me that I speak with someone here. I shall be thankful if you will have someone come out to meet me."

I spoke with Simon Peter, and he and James and John descended the stair and I alongside them. As they and the stranger met, he said, "You men, I believe, are followers of the one crucified. Is this true?"

Somewhat apprehensively, but with full firmness, the apostles asserted their discipleship. Then the stranger said, "I am pleased and honored that you speak with me. As you know, I am Roman. My name is Marcus Gracian, and it was I who commanded the hundred the day your Jesus died. After more than thirty years of service with Caesar's legions, I have now resigned my commission. Tomorrow I leave Jerusalem to take a ship at Joppa for my return to Rome. Before I go, I must know more of him whom we crucified. What can you tell me? What is the meaning of him?"

Peter, ordinarily glib of speech, silently turned to the other two. John hesitated as though searching for a proper reply. At last it was James who spoke: "We welcome your coming, sir, and your question. As for answering it, I scarcely know where to begin or how. Come with us and sit and let us talk."

The Roman's response came quickly: "This I cannot do.

I am unworthy of your hospitality. I have observed the comings and goings on yonder stair, and I do not merit a place in company such as yours. But I must know more of him whom we crucified. Who was he really?"

Again the apostles hesitated, and after a few moments the Roman again spoke: "I am sure you must have known him well. Please tell me, if you can."

In deep earnestness, the soldier looked pleadingly and penetratingly from face to face, awaiting an answer.

After some silence, John spoke: "Indeed, yes, we knew him well..." Seemingly poised to go on, he fell abruptly silent. Then he said, "But to speak the whole truth, I am not sure we now know him we once believed we knew. We strive to comprehend."

"As, in fact, I also do," the Roman said. "I too strive to understand. From you I had hoped for a clear and easy answer. Perhaps I hoped too much. It may be that nothing is clear and easy when we get to the deep of things. And perhaps in pondering this Jesus, we go as deep as mortals ever can."

John had listened carefully and now he said, "I do not yet comprehend the meaning of it, and I speak for myself only, but I can tell you this: If Jesus is merely man, then I am somewhat less."

The Roman reacted with a start. "So also have I come to think," he replied. "I suppose him somewhere beyond us all. But however far into the dimness I need go, I shall seek him, and so I think will you. As you seek him in your way I shall seek him in mine, and when we have found him I feel that we, Roman and Jew, will be together there. Thank you for seeing me. I leave you now."

Marcus Gracian turned and walked away, alone. And the three apostles, in soul-wrenching dismay, stood silently on the street.

Peter was first to speak: "The man came with a question,

and we had not the wisdom to answer him."

It was then with heavy hearts and troubled minds that the men ascended the stair. On the terrace John turned solemnly to the others, saying, "Consider what is happening here: This Roman, in his quest, does for us again what the woman Ashabel in hers has done for us once already. Like her, he compels us to find answers for those who seek them."

Here John paused, then looking penetratingly into the eyes of his two companions, he continued slowly in an inquiring tone: "Or perhaps he compels us to find expression for answers we deeply know we already have."

Pausing again, his voice almost a whisper now and speaking as though to himself, he added: "Or maybe he compels us to find the courage to make known these answers to a world that has never heard such truth before."

The three stood silent for a while, each somewhere in the depths of his own thought, and then the silence was broken by James, saying simply, "Let us go in."

The men were about to move on into the room when Simon Peter momentarily restrained the others, speaking quietly: "My brothers, it is not only the Roman and the woman from Magdala whose voices we hear. There is yet a third: Mary, the mother of our Lord. All speak the same word: A necessity is laid upon us. Nor, I think, can we escape it."

"No, Simon, we cannot. Of course we cannot, nor should we try." It was James who said this and with that the three walked silently into the room.

V

At nightfall on this day, as on most, numbers present at the room diminished greatly. As the lamps were lit and the evening moved on into night, it was apparent that only a few would remain throughout.

By the third hour of night, only four apostles were present and none of the other disciples. Those present were the four fishermen of Galilee. Seated at the table, two at one end and one nearby on either side, light from the table lamps glistening in their eyes served only to accent the fatigue that lined their faces.

From my place on my pallet on the floor, the four appeared as a tableau that has lingered indelibly in my memory. While most scenes fade with passing time, this, for me, has only grown more vivid.

Here were James and John and Simon Peter and Andrew, two pairs of brothers, lifetime friends and associates, who had long known each other well. Now three years past, hearing the summons of Jesus, they had left their ships, their livelihood, and their families to follow him, not knowing how long the journey might be.

Initially supposing the time would be short, it had stretched to a year, and then two, and now three. During these years, these four and all the others had thought much about homes and families, longing to return, but there had been a compelling quality about him they followed.

While any might have returned to their fishing at any time, none had. To be sure, certain others who had followed for a while had from time to time gone back to former pursuits, difficulties of the way proving more rigorous than they were willing to endure.

But not these four. From the Great Sea eastward to Perea

beyond the Jordan, and from Mount Hermon in the north to the southern limits of Judea, they had followed as the Master led. In their journeys they commonly had no advance knowledge of where they would next go or of what they might encounter there.

They had dealt with throngs that everywhere gathered around, some respectfully and some to jeer. They had endured curious gazes and sometimes spiteful stares as they trekked through strange places. They had wrestled with hostilities and conspiracies, they had felt fear as lawyers tried to entrap Jesus in what he did or said, they had stood by in dread as schemers undertook to undo him.

Discipleship had not been easy. These were proud and modestly prosperous men who had left their business affairs with hired servants to embrace a journey into the unknown. Often of necessity they had begged for food or shelter, beseeching aid of strangers. Sometimes there had been neither food nor shelter, and at night they had lain famished and cold beneath the stars or underneath the overhanging clouds of the former or latter rain. But they had followed on.

These disciples, and others with them, had carefully observed all that Jesus did and had intently listened to all he said. As opportunity allowed, they had spoken of all this among themselves, often reviewing the day at the day's end, recounting marvels they had seen and remarkable things they had heard. Frequently some wrote of things remembered, then compared notations and speculated as to reasons and meanings.

All this time, as months and years went by, these followers had walked the hill-country roads, the village streets, and the great city thoroughfares, never fully understanding him they followed and never knowing to what destination he might eventually lead them. But they had believed in him and hoped for something good and great.

Then suddenly, only seven weeks ago, all things had

converged into crisis. Enemies of Jesus had at last marshaled all their powers against him. He had died, and these pilgrims had believed the pilgrimage finished; the arduous quest had come to naught. Then having witnessed their Leader alive again, there was, after all, hope.

But now he was gone. And in their pilgrimage across the mountains and valleys of hopefulness, they had come again to a valley, this the deepest and darkest of them all. Although they knew their Lord alive, they were lost in a wilderness of unknowns. Yet, beyond the darkness, these four, together with certain others, were seeing a glimmer of light, ill-defined as yet, but swelling somewhat.

Something is there, they were saying to one another, but what is it? Whatever, it must surely be that for which Jesus lived and died and to which he called us at the first. Certainly he did not summon us to these years of pilgrimage only to die and leave us stranded here. Before his death, we never understood his ultimate aim. We supposed this and we supposed that, and on the day he died this truth was made clear: Whatever his ultimate aim, it lay somewhere beyond all our supposings, and there it still lies.

Their thought continued: We are in post-mortem time, and we have this advantage now. To the sum of all we had known of Jesus, his death has now been added. Now we must see all of that in the new light of this. Events since his dying seem to say that his death was as extraordinary as was his life. As he was wont to use all occasions as a means to some end, so also without doubt he has used his death. But to what end? This we must know and this we must pursue to the very limits of sense.

After the years of pilgrimage and these recent weeks of mystery, it was to this awesome moment that the four fishermen of Galilee had now come. And here, late this night, near exhaustion, in the yellow light of flickering lamps, they would strive with issues beyond the normal range of mind.

It was apparent the men had not planned this gathering. It was as though each had deeply felt a need for the others, and therefore all had tarried and assembled here. It was clear, likewise, that there was no advance plan for events that would follow.

As I remember, it all began with James, who wearily sighed, closed his eyes, and reflectively said, "O God, you are my God; I seek you; my soul thirsts for you; my flesh faints for you, as in a dry and thirsty land...."

Others followed then, each in turn, speaking the language of Israel's ancient songs: "Why are you cast down, O my soul, and why are you disquieted within me? Hope in God; for I shall yet praise him.... I trust in you, O Lord; I say: You are my God; my times are in your hand.... O send forth your light and your truth; let them lead me."

It was Simon Peter then who initiated a dialogue that would continue far beyond the midnight hour. I heard all of it, but it was only I who did, and my memories therefore are wholly my own. Although I have had these many years to relive this night in memory, it is only sparingly that I attempt to tell of it now.

Reflectively and pensively, Simon Peter said: "I understand fishing. I know the way of handling ships and managing nets. I know where the schools of fish are and their habits of migration season by season. I can read the weather signs and tell about calm times and storms. But all this that has happened of late — my mind staggers beneath the weight of it. This plain fisherman yearns for the mental powers of a great philosopher."

James responded: "I suppose there is much, Simon, that none of us understand. Perhaps we never shall. We may as well accept it as truth. God has uniquely expressed himself in Jesus. In a way that stands as singular in all time; God has lately moved among us. And when God moves in, ought we not expect some disruption of the ordinary?"

One of the others, Andrew I think, said: "I hear you saying that in Jesus we look upon dimensions beyond our measuring and that we have no measuring stick for sizing them, no scale to weigh them on, and no standard to view them by."

Again Peter: "Do you suppose that even the skilled mind of the most learned could comprehend all this that we four have seen and heard?"

It was John who answered: "This I doubt. Do you recall the legend of the stone? The stone was large, very large and of enormous weight, and there was a contest among strong men to determine who might lift it. One by one they tried, each in his turn, from the smallest to the greatest. All failed, all equally failed. The strongest was able to move it not one whit more than the weakest. You see, all of us are alike when we lay hold of something big enough. And I am persuaded that in the Jesus event we do lay hold of something precisely this big. Doesn't this mean that any one of us four is as qualified to deal with all this as the wisest and most learned of men?"

One of the others, which I do not remember, said: "Of course. And it also means that we ought not wish to be philosophers but rather to fulfill our role as ordinary men."

John again: "After all, life's deepest regions are never sounded by mind, but by spirit. Nor are its heights perceived by intellect, but rather discovered by the aspiring soul. Actually, the mind's range of competence is narrow, isn't it? It occupies a thin band of the somewhat familiar and lies between the unplumbed depths below and the unshared heights above. Venturing into these awaits a movement of spirit, a questing of soul."

Andrew said: "A thought comes and the thought is this: A rose will communicate its beauty only to one who sees. Appreciation will glean from it what probing never could. Beauty has direct access to spirit, and in its coming may bypass the mind. We may fully enjoy the beauty of a flower and yet never understand all that makes it grow. I think he is self-deprived and poor who will admit into his life only that which can squeeze through the narrow gate of the mind."

James said thoughtfully: "Then let us not grieve that we are ordinary. The loftiest truth and the finest of beauty belong to people who feel. Great intellect and deep misery may keep close company, and one who is of common mind may be most whole."

Peter again: "We are saying, aren't we, that it is not required of us that we understand everything?"

To this John responded: "Certainly so, and I think this also needs to be said: Among the compartments of our thought, we ought always to leave some spaces for the unknown. If we close all our doors, we become prisoners of the commonplace."

Then one of the others said: "And do you not think that as we humans, however learned, arrange our catalogue of truths, we ought to reserve a place for truth yet to be discovered? I think so."

To this John replied: "How vain of anyone to argue that a thing cannot exist merely because we are unable to observe it or to reason that a thing cannot happen because we do not understand it. Could they speak, even our household pets could counter that. After all, some of them can hear sounds we cannot hear and see things we cannot see... Oh how vast is this dome under which we of humankind live out these years of ours!"

Here the four fell silent for a few moments. Then suddenly Simon Peter smiled broadly, a sparkle flashing in his eyes. It was good to see Peter smile. Glancing about pleasantly to the others, he said, "And were we saying there are no philosophers among us? Were we listening and others speaking, this conversation would probably impress us as profoundly philosophical!"

There were now smiles all around, and James said somewhat bemusedly, "We have rather surprised ourselves, haven't we?"

To this John responded: "Perhaps discovered ourselves! 'Discovered' — this may be a better word. We believed ourselves fishermen; we assumed that we were; and perhaps all this while we have never known who we really are."

I have thought many years about this that John said. Is it possible we may move through a lifetime, never wholly realizing life? Perhaps. After all, these men were the same four who had labored together at the lake in Galilee, and there they had believed they knew themselves — and one another. Perhaps, calling them, Jesus had seen in them something they never knew was there and would never have known had they not responded to his call.

Maybe most of what we see of others is but reflection. Circumstance bears in upon them, and what we see is the way they reflect it back. In different circumstances we see different reflections, and it is only when we have seen another in many and varied circumstances that we begin to know who the other really is. Likewise, we scarcely know who we ourselves are until we see ourselves responding to that which bears in upon us. Perhaps it was only with the coming of Jesus and his impact upon their lives that these men began to find out who they really were.

These four had known themselves in a community of ships and nets. They had more recently been catapulted into another world. For them, this new world was a strange and mysterious one for which they had felt inadequate and ill-prepared, with each, I think, feeling somewhat alone.

Tonight there were no ships, no nets. The familiar shores of Galilee were a long way off and the familiar voice of Jesus was no longer heard. Near this midnight hour in this great, dark place, haggard faces showing in a small circle of lamp-light, the men wrestled with such thoughts as certainly must have pushed each mind to its tether's end and beyond. But here, in circumstances unlike any had ever known before, they were together and they knew it and deeply felt it. I think that not one of them felt alone anymore.

As together when fishermen they could cope with Galilean storms, so now as disciples they were gathering resources of mind and spirit to deal with whatever discipleship might mean. Thus, here at this midnight time these pairs of brothers were brought together in a bond that, as time would prove, could withstand all storms that might later rage against it.

For the four, this was a moment of great rejoicing and for the future it was an instance of great importance. While I think it meant much to all of them, I am sure it meant the most to Peter. From this time, the man was as one inspired. I have always thought of this nighttime moment as one of the brightest and most significant in the whole of the ten days.

Other significant moments, however, would follow in the hours of this night.

Picking up on John's thought relative to self-discovery, Andrew said, "Have we a new identity now? As we have known ourselves as fishermen, we now know ourselves as disciples."

Then, as an afterthought, he added, "But what is a disciple? Do we know? What does it mean to be one? And the difference between being and not being — what is this? Becoming a disciple — this new identity — what does it mean? What difference does it make?"

Peter, still in smiling voice, spoke in mock reproachfulness: "There, there, Andrew, you are being a philosopher again!"

Then in a more serious vein, John said, "How can the man avoid it? How can we all? Sometimes philosophers are made by circumstance; some subjects may be so deep that they make philosophers of all who touch them. I think there is no doubt of it. In these days, we are very much in touch with a deepness that will make philosophers of many for many years yet coming."

At this, the countenance of Simon Peter changed instantly. The light of amusement faded from his eyes and a serenity seemed to possess him. He said, "John, what you have just said is the echo of a thing I have been thinking."

In the excitement of these last moments, the four apostles had bounded from their places and were now standing about. Motioning them to their chairs again, Peter continued: "Since his death, we have struggled with great diligence to understand Jesus. Why? Mostly I feel to satisfy our own private need to understand. We have been personally discomforted by the mystery of him. Not knowing where these recent developments have taken us or where we now stand, we feel a profound uneasiness. It is chiefly, I suspect, for our own sakes that we strive to clear away all questions concerning him. Do I speak fairly?"

The others affirming the probable truth of Peter's comment, he then went on: "I think we have been wrong in this and perhaps selfish. The thought that occurs to me is this: Perhaps we disciples of Jesus have an obligation to others, perhaps a very great obligation, perhaps to many others. Jesus said to us, 'I have chosen you.' The question is: For what? Are we ourselves his only purpose? Does his intention end with us? Or has he a purpose beyond us? And if beyond, how far beyond? I have come to believe, my brothers, that his purpose reaches to all Israel. If this be so, then an enormous obligation is upon us."

"I see your meaning, Simon," replied James, "and I see your thought concerning obligation as both an important and a disturbing one. May it be that Jesus is counting on us to carry forward that which he has begun?"

"Indeed," said John, "I believe it so. But whatever this is that he has begun, I believe it not for Israel only, but for all people everywhere and perhaps for all time."

All eyes turned to John with all voices silent. At last Peter spoke incredulously, "John, are you saying that Jesus has begun something that will affect the entire world?"

Thoughtfully silent for a few moments, John then replied, "Yes. I... I am saying this and I believe it is true. I am confident that Jesus has brought something new into the world. I feel that somehow he has released a mighty force; I feel this strongly. It is deep within me and very real. But I have been unable to snare it with any net of mind. Nor have I been able, therefore, to capture it with any net of language. You know how it is: Some fish are too small for our nets and some are too large. I suppose I want to hold this up as we would a prize catch beneath the Galilean sun. But it remains somewhere in the deep, a realism without form and without name."

John paused, as if pondering what next to say. Looking earnestly from face to face, he then said, "I have not spoken of this before and it really seems too much mine to share it now, but I do with you, blood of my blood and friends, for I am confident you will hear me — sympathetically?"

About the table all nodded silently, none speaking. John continued: "I am as one who has received a most precious gift. I know it to be unlike anything I have ever seen or touched before, but I cannot determine what it is. It comes from a cherished friend, and therefore it means much to me. I long to tell others about it but have no language for the telling. Deeply, my brothers, I am sure of this: Jesus has added something priceless and highly important to the world's wealth of life and spirit. This I feel but cannot define."

John's tone was one of awe, and now in like tone Peter responded: "By his life, death, and return from death, what has Jesus done? This is the question, isn't it? In the quest for the answer, all of us are together with you, John."

Remembering words heard from Jesus, Andrew said quietly, "Ask and you will receive; seek and you will find;

knock and it will be opened for you."

Drifting away that night into sleep, the last I heard was the calm, assured voice of Simon Peter evenly ascending to God in prayer.

Many have been the times in these years after when I could have wished my sleep to come to me as it came that night. For many days have been filled with trouble, with suffering our people have been required to endure. Many days have brought news of floggings, imprisonments, and deaths of good people who had committed no crime but to follow and love our Lord. When the next blow might fall, or where, has been ever a reason for great distress.

How soothing in the anxiety of these troubled nighttimes to have heard again the praying voice of Simon. Only this once, though, was this privilege ever mine. Thus did a night that moved me deeply conclude with a benediction that rests upon me still.

VI

It was at about the fifth hour of a generally unsettled day when the Zealot, alone as was not uncommon for him, trudged wearily up the stair. For this sorely afflicted apostle, these late weeks had been a difficult time. Generally disturbed in spirit and mind, he was often deeply so.

First had been his disappointment in Jesus. He had believed the Lord would deliver Israel from Rome, but Rome yet ruled. That bereavement is especially onerous that comes from having seen a cherished hope writhing in the throes of death. This sight the Zealot had been unable to put out of mind.

Then, too, he had seen lesser hopes meet like fates, particularly with the unmaskings of Zebulon Brashabe and Banis Barodis. Bidding farewell to an illusion can be a painful parting. And this pain the Zealot had deeply felt.

Now, plodding upward tread by tread, he walked as though the weight of worlds was on him. It was clear to all who saw him that the burden he carried was great, or that at least he believed it to be. Several sympathetically gathered around, offering support.

Responding hungrily to the outreach of these who cared, the tortured disciple opened his heart to them. Although it was with difficulty and under strain of deep emotion that the Zealot spoke, it was apparent that he welcomed the attentive ears of these who stood about him. I think he deeply needed to tell these others of the things that troubled him.

He said, "I have come just now from the place Iscariot died." I am confident that in all the days until now this was the first mention of Iscariot's name.

Suppressing a sob, the Zealot continued: "I stood today at the brink of Hinnom where our brother roped himself to the limb of an ancient olive. I looked long at the ragged cliff down which the broken limb and the broken body fell. I had to go there. I had to see. I had to know. I think I had to feel some of the pain he felt. And I think I do. He was my friend."

The speaker's voice failed completely. For a moment all were silent. Then came a voice, whose I cannot recall, that blurted words with a tinge of anger in them: "I have tried to forget that man; the memory of him is a thorn for me." The outburst was ignored.

Now that attention was drawn to Judas Iscariot, a weighty discussion followed. One asked: "Is it true — that he took his own life?"

Quickly, another added, "Why?"

Thomas responded, "Why? I suppose because of this awful thing he did."

"Awful thing? What was this?" asked Matthias.

"The kiss," Thomas replied.

"Yes, the kiss. I know of it. But what is it that makes a kiss an awful thing?" asked Matthias, persistently pursuing the matter.

Thomas replied, "A kiss is a way of saying something. There are times when kisses say improper things, and this one did. A kiss is not in every instance an expression of love; sometimes it is a way of doing a reprehensible thing and this one was."

"My dear Thomas," said Mathias softly and evenly, "do we really know what it was that by that kiss Judas meant to do? I am led to wonder."

Since his initial mention of Iscariot the Zealot had remained quiet, listening, but with a vexation building within him.

Suddenly, with great intensity, he spoke: "Oh my brothers, you must understand this, within a hairline, it was I who bestowed that kiss!"

Astonishment swept through the company. Then one asked, "Simon, what is this that you are saying?"

His tone more calm now, the Zealot replied, "Iscariot and I were kindred of mind and spirit. He believed, as did I, that Jesus would re-establish the kingdom in Israel. Waiting for this, he was impatient, as was I. Together we observed all the signs, longing to see a signal, anxious that Jesus would quickly make his move against Rome. But he long delayed.

"Then came those Passover days, and the authorities were closing in. It seemed to us that if Jesus were ever to act, the time for action had come. We could not believe that Jesus would ever allow them to take him. I am certain of this: When our brother Judas arranged the confrontation in Gethsemane that night, he was confident that the garden would be instantly visited by an angelic host with swords, wreaking havoc among priests and Romans.

"Judas meant, I think, to precipitate a war, the outcome of which he had no doubt. His intention was to create a crisis, firmly convinced that when it came to this, Jesus would assert himself and that his awesome powers would be more than sufficient to crush the might of Rome."

The Zealot paused, then added thoughtfully, "But Judas was mistaken about Jesus. I know this now. He did not understand him. Nor did I. Nor do I yet, I fear. I now know what Jesus was not, but I have yet to understand what he was."

The Zealot had spoken quietly, thoughtfully, and with no employment of his left forearm. As he concluded, several men closed around him to embrace and offer reassurance.

There would be further discussion of Judas Iscariot. There were those who could not view the man as the Zealot had portrayed him. Philip would say, "Dealing with disillusionment can be difficult. It may be that near the end Judas saw Jesus as making his unexpected turn, and perhaps disenchanted, he lost hope. It can be only a short way from hopelessness to hostility."

71

Thomas would say, "I need to think more of this."

Consideration of Judas would provoke profound thought. Essentially, the issue was this: Had the man intended harm for Jesus, or had he rather believed that no harm could possibly come to him? Had he wholly mistrusted Jesus, or had he actually trusted him more than any of the others and believed in him more deeply? While never resolved, the question of Iscariot was never, however, a divisive one among the disciples.

Inconclusive as all speculations were, there was never doubt of this: Two apostles had been gravely disappointed in Jesus. The one, Judas Iscariot, had expressed his disappointment in one way, and now the other, Simon the Zealot, would deal with his in another.

There was, however, an important difference between the one circumstance and the other. Iscariot had acted alone and impulsively; he had gone to his death with no consoling word from a friend and no comforting arm about his shoulders. But not the Zealot. As he struggled to find his way out of the quagmire of his bewilderment, he found himself consolingly surrounded by fellow-beings, sometimes as bewildered as he, but forgiving, loving, caring, and sharing a common quest.

When we come to life's dark places, how meaningful is the comfort that others often are! It may be good at times to wander alone among the cedars of Lebanon or the dunes of Arabia, but at length there is nothing better than the sight of another face or the touch of another hand or the sound of another voice. The heart's vague hunger is satisfied at last only in the meeting of person with person, only in the beating of heart with heart. Deep within, there is our need for one another, and this need is the bond that binds us. Thank God for others, the human and divine, and when at length all human faces fade, there is always God.

There is never a rule for measuring what one may mean

to another. I think no one will ever know how much his fellow disciples meant to the Zealot in his struggle up from despair. Step by step, as the occasion required, they drew him out and brought him along, until eventually they would share a triumph that was a joy for all.

As I think of him now, I look upon the Zealot as a rare and complex person. In depression, it was his wont to withdraw, and yet he seemed ever ready to reach for any hand that was outreached to him. Although he required solitude, he was irresistibly drawn to the company of his fellows.

With the Zealot, sincerity was a passion. There was nothing of the hypocritical about him. The windows of his soul were always open and there were no locks on his doors. He was a scroll unrolled for all to read, and he was as honest with himself as he was open and honest with others.

Although at one time or another he suffered certain illusions, to be illusionary was wholly foreign to all he was. The illusions he entertained he strongly held as truth. For him, change never came easily, and his struggles of soul were at levels deeper than most.

Starting as a patriot and lover of country, he had looked on Jesus as a means of freedom for his people. It was a rough and rock-riddled road he traveled from there to gain the pinnacle of faith on which at last he stood. In this pilgrimage, he owed much to those who were with him on the way. This he knew, and for this, in all the years after, he remained sincerely thankful.

At the present, though, he grieved for a friend, and viewing the scene of Iscariot's death had brought him no relief. However, pouring out his heart sincerely to these around him, he had compelled the company to consider Judas, and this was needful. They would afterward wrestle long in thought and prayer over the puzzle and paradoxes of this strange man, but they would never understand him. Most felt the loss of him, among them Simon Peter, but none more deeply than the Zealot.

Peter was a magnanimous man. Big of heart and kind of spirit, trustful and forgiving, he embodied qualities that endeared him to others. Heartily outgoing and given to enthusiasm, it was his way to believe readily and act decisively.

The man was a paragon of energy and vigor. Had a ship been impaled the seashore, it was he who would have leaped overboard to dislodge it. In the matter of work, he would do more than two of most other men, and this not so much because of physical strength as because of the spirited way he went about everything he did.

He was a volatile fellow, a man of action, quick to speak and often borne on the tide of his own enthusiasms. His spirit was host to powerful feelings, and he could at times be carried away by them. Sometimes extreme in the things he did or said, he had more than once stirred the animosity of others around him.

Some people, though, are easier to forgive than others, and Peter was one of these. So magnanimous of spirit was he that others found it difficult to hold much against him for any great length of time. Caught in the complex emotion of recent Passover events, he had acted at times impulsively and rashly. But during the weeks following, most disciples had seen so much of the noble and the generous in the man that distasteful memories had generally faded away. And now, during the upper room gatherings, he had risen in stature until none stood taller.

It was virtually inevitable, I think, that some member of the company would emerge as the leader. Looking back on it now, I suppose it was also inevitable that this leader should have been Simon Peter.

Among the Eleven, none were highly educated or of great wealth, but all were men of rare quality. Ordinary with respect to status, as status is normally measured, they were extraordinary in matters of perceptivity and basic intelligence. I always thought it remarkable that Jesus could have found so many such men in the small quarter of Galilee from which most came. Of course, by the time I knew them they had traveled three years with him, and this may have made an enormous difference.

Among these, exceptional as they were, Simon Peter, unstable as he sometimes seemed to be, easily and naturally drifted into a position of leadership. Among the company, the alluring qualities of the man were more than enough to overcome the vulnerability that was sometimes so distressingly apparent in him.

Now that Simon Peter stood with such stature among the apostles, it was perhaps inevitable that he would speak at some length of their singular fellowship, the ties that bound them, the road over which they had together come, and their unique relationship with their Lord. There were then among them for a while expressions of comradeship and sentiment, with memories shared, occasional tears, and a smile now and then.

The mood, though, was somewhat amended as my uncle spoke. He said, "As we think of this apostleship, I offer a question that has lately been much on my mind: For what purpose did Jesus select us twelve? What for and why us?"

It appeared at first that several were about to answer him, but as though suddenly unsure, all hesitated. Answers often come easily that come of first thought, but afterthoughts tend to complicate answers. So was it now. The question that at the asking seemed simple became troublesome when further considered.

When at length the disciples began a discussion of it, I believe the questions were more numerous than the answers: His reason for choosing us — was it friendship only, or was there another? Was it because in some way he needed us, or because we needed him, or was it both or neither? Was he all this while preparing us to share some way in his teaching or otherwise in his work? If this be so, what is now our thing to do? If we shall teach, what shall we teach?

"What shall we teach?" echoed one of the apostles, which I cannot be sure, although I believe either Matthew or Nathanael. "What shall we teach? An essential question, is it not? I think of the Great Prophet and his witness to God's call: 'A voice said cry.' But Isaiah was not satisfied with this. He asked, 'What shall I cry?' A messenger must have a message, else his mission is in vain. It is not enough to feel a need for crying. It is one thing to feel that something should be said, but it is quite another to know what to say. Just now, it may be that we are somewhere between the feeling and the knowing. Is there a message that calls for delivery? We all know there is, don't we? But what is it? What shall we cry? This is the treasure we seek."

To this Philip added: "Ours is the task of drawing water from a well that is very deep with ropes that are too short."

"Then we should tie our ropes together and let the bucket down deeper," someone said, and whether lightheartedly or seriously I have never known.

"And behold all the while, as we fumble with ropes and buckets, perhaps the water is rising." This from John, and I am sure quite seriously spoken.

Following a short conversation with James and John, Simon Peter addressed the other apostles and all the assembly: "Over and over, again and again, in and about this room, we find ourselves asking: What is it that our Lord wills for us? What would he have us do? The question is for today and for all tomorrows. Our needs are many, and important among them is our need that he instruct us. No longer do we see him or hear him, but once we did. Lodged in our many memories are long scrolls of things he once said. Perhaps our understanding of him and what he wishes of us now is best to be had by hearing again what he said to us then.

"Therefore, I offer a suggestion. Let each of us try seriously to recall all that we ever heard Jesus say. Especially, let us search our memories for that which may relate to himself and to us in our relationship with him."

The suggestion of Peter was heartily received. Apparently, he had given voice to a thought already in many minds. Peter then added: "Let us then, all of us, think of this today and tonight, and then with the dawning of tomorrow, we shall pull such pieces as we may from our memories and lay them out in some order for all to see."

The prospect pleasing to all, it was an animated and effusive band of disciples who bade God's peace one to another and sought their host homes as the day came to its close.

VII

Following Simon Peter's assignment given to the disciples yesterday, today an aura of excitement seemed to pervade the company. Many came early to the room. The sun was yet concealed somewhere beyond the Kidron when the earliest to arrive came up the stair.

Until now, the mood of many had been dominated by the waiting. Today these who waited would undertake a task, and it was stimulating to anticipate the doing.

When most were gathered, Simon Peter placed a sheaf of parchments on the table and announced, "The parchments are clean, never touched by ink or pen. They are for the recording of our memories." He then asked Philip and Nathanael to write as much as possible of things remembered.

The two apostles agreed, Philip adding, "And, Simon, perhaps you know that for more than two years I have often put to parchment certain sayings of our Lord." Here he reached into his garment, withdrew a bundle of parchments, and carefully placed them alongside the others.

With this, there were a number of the apostles and certain other disciples who revealed possession of occasional writings they had made and kept, most to be sure, only minimal in scope. The record of Philip, however, much more complete, has in years following been read and used by many, among these both John and John Mark.

Peter was indeed aware of Philip's earlier writing. All in fact, knowing Philip well, had understood this most timid of the apostles to be of somewhat scholarly mind. He spoke three languages proficiently and knew more of the Greek and Indic philosophies than any of the others. Although his timidity was often construed as ineptitude, this quiet apostle's mind flowed as does the calm stream that is great in depth.

Although one of the oldest among the Twelve and John the very youngest, it was alongside Philip that John most often walked when the group had trudged the long trails city to city throughout the land.

Now, as I have said, had come a day of purpose and therefore a day of hope, and with the hope, the excitement. The disciples would undertake together to relive the years and rewalk the trails, trying to hear again the Master's voice. They would attempt to combine memories, the better to comprehend him with whom they had walked this while.

John said, "We heard him as things were. If we can hear him again, it will be as things are. We saw him in the light that was then ours, but the light in which we see him is different now. Events have intervened; we are now this side of a death and a resurrection. His words that seemed to bear one message then may come to us with another message now."

John finishing, his brother then said, "Simon and John and I believe we have a message for you from Jesus."

Before James could continue, the room erupted with excitement, astonishment, and a varied mix of questions.

"Please hear, men," James called out above the uproar, "please hear me carefully." Then he asked for quiet and the full and thoughtful attention of all.

When at last the room subsided into silence, James continued: "The message we have is from a long while ago, given to us then to be delivered, we think, to you at this time. It was confided in secrecy, and according to his instruction, we are ready to reveal it now. Simon —"

Here James turned to Peter, gesturing that he proceed. This Simon did, saying, "It was near Caesarea Philippi, and many will remember the place. The time was near the first hour of the day and the sun was barely risen. Jesus spoke to the three of us, asking that we walk with him to a place apart. Some will remember the occasion."

There were nods and glances from person to person, as

there were indeed those who remembered.

Peter continued: "The three of us, with Jesus, were a long while gone. Ascending a mountain near the base of Hermon, Jesus walked slowly and silently, as in meditation, we following, nor did we in any way disturb or distract him. Until near the third hour he said nothing. By that time we had climbed well upward, reaching a high elevation. Still without speaking, Jesus turned, glanced pleasantly toward us, and then in turn looked seriously and intently into the eyes of each of us..."

Tears had crept into the big man's voice, and his big heart torn with feeling, the voice now failed completely. He turned entreatingly to John, who stood beside him. The young apostle reached up, laid a hand momentarily on Simon's shoulder, and went on with the story: "What we saw was near unbearable to see and is near impossible to tell. As we three stood looking, Jesus slowly lifted his head and raised his eyes skyward. Without other motion, he seemed to rise a little above the ground, and his countenance changed, assuming a serenity and a beauty unlike any ever seen. There was a white glow about him, a radiance so bright that the surrounding sunlight was dimmed by the light of it.

"Then appeared two others who stood beside him, the one on the one side and the other on the other, and they spoke with him and the language was strange to us. Then we heard a voice coming down from somewhere above, the language ours, but the voice unlike any we had ever heard. The voice said, 'This is my beloved son.' It was a voice from God; we are sure of this.

"Certainly that was a holy place, a holy time. As one, we three fell on our faces. After how long we have never known, Jesus came and touched us. He was quite himself now. As we looked up to him, he smiled and said, 'Do not be afraid, my friends, and do arise.'

"As we looked about, we saw that only Jesus was there,

and as we arose, he said quite pleasantly, 'Come now, let us go to the others.'

"As we walked, descending the mountain, Jesus was a long while silent again. At length he stopped, saying, 'Wait.' Then after a moment he said with great earnestness, 'Tell no one what you have seen and heard today — not until after I am dead and risen from the dead. Then you may; I desire that you do, and you will know the time.' "

As John ceased speaking, James said, "We believe the time has come. We think that on that Ulathan mountain that day Jesus foresaw our needs of these days. As we search for signs that may help us understand him, he provides this one. By this foretoken of his glory, he draws aside a curtain that we may see. Now that we know him risen, I think he desires all of us to see him as we three saw him then. And to hear the voice we heard."

Peter, having regained his composure, now said: "This, dear ones, is our report to you, delivered as he desired. Great is our privilege to have seen what we saw, and great is our privilege in being his messengers to you now. Sometimes mere words cannot say all we may wish them to, and this is notable among such times; we know this. Perhaps you have questions?"

Since Peter's first reference to the event in Ulatha, the entire assembly had been immobile, raptly attentive, and overwhelmed by a spirit of reverence. That spirit now continued to prevail and there was a long interval before anyone spoke. Then it was Thomas, I believe, who said, "You whose own the experience was, tell us please what you believe it means."

John replied, his voice attuned to the hush that prevailed: "One thing is sure, I believe, perhaps two: It was not as a surprise that death came to Jesus, and he knew beforehand that death could not ultimately hold him in its power."

James added, "The plans of men normally terminate with

death; the plan of Jesus included it. Apparently he looked upon death and resurrection as pivotal in his life, dividing it into two segments, before and after."

Peter said, "I think we see that beyond apparent reality is a deeper one." Then turning to James and John, he added, "Perhaps one or both of you may choose to speak more of this."

James responded: "All of us, I believe, had long supposed Jesus the Messiah. We, like all Israel, had pre-formed our image of what the Messiah should be and do. That image did not include a crucifixion. It is only in these last awesome weeks that we had come to understand that Jesus did not conform to the image we made. The issue now is this: Do we hold to our image and wait for a later Messiah, or do we abandon the image and accept Jesus as he?

"May it be that those of Israel who looked most eagerly for the Messiah to come did not know him when he came? May it be that Jesus was he and that when he came they killed him? And why? Not because he failed to rise to the level of their expectations, but because he went so far beyond them. Perhaps he was so much more than they expected him to be that they could not believe that he was he. If Israel's image of the Messiah was defective, so was ours. Messiah is more than we had assumed; we know this now. What more and how much more — this is the deep unknown, and to explore it is the task that stands before us."

These were weighty words, and while they fell on willing ears, the minds to which they came staggered beneath the weight of them. As James concluded, it appeared for a while that no one would speak. At last Thomas reflectively offered this: "Yes, had Jesus followed the messianic road we had mapped for him, we would now know where we are. And where would this be? At the end of a failed enterprise. But since he took an unscheduled turn, we know not where we are or where he would have us go. The questions are twin:

What is his purpose, and therefore what shall be ours?"

"Thomas, you have summed it well." It was Simon Peter who said this, and then he continued: "Is there any doubt in any mind that Jesus is our Messiah?"

It was the Zealot who answered firmly and strongly: "There is no doubt in my mind." As he spoke, a wave of rejoicing swept over the room and two or three nearby swept the man into their arms. The joy was for the long strides the Zealot had made and for an evident abatement of the storm that had raged within him.

In a tone somewhat judicial, Simon Peter announced: "Is it understood amongst us, then, that we firmly and finally hold it as truth — our Lord Jesus is the Messiah?"

About the room there were everywhere sounds of assent: "It is true... We do... We hold it to be so."

"So be it," said Peter.

Apart from the single comment of Thomas, only Peter, James, and John had spoken in the assembly on this day. At this point, however, another voice would be heard, which was that of the reticent and timid Philip. This smallest of the apostles arose from his place at the table, stood as tall as his dwarfish stature would allow, and said somewhat apologetically: "For many days a sound has run through my mind like a song. And the sound is a word. May I tell you about it? Yes, Jesus is Messiah, and Messiah is ruler, Messiah is king, and kings are anointed into their kingships. I see Jesus as one anointed, not by the hand or authority of man, but of God. In the Greek language there is a wonderful word. To me, there is the sound of music in it. Like a refrain that will not die away, it keeps ringing within me. The word is *christos*, and it means one who is anointed, a king. I look upon our Lord Jesus as one anointed. He is our king, our *Christos*."

When Philip spoke, I am sure that he had no idea of the commotion and high emotion his modest comment would stir. "Praise God!" someone shouted, and the room erupted in a tumult of rejoicing.

Philip appeared surprised, even startled. It was as though he saw no connection between anything he may have said and all the commotion it caused. As he turned to resume his place at the table, he was set upon by many who closed in to thank and applaud him. Although at first confused by all this, the realization gradually came to him that his plain word of witness was infinitely more significant than he knew.

As calm slowly returned, various conversations took shape about the room. Royalty — anointing — kingship — kingdom — after all, had not Jesus spoken often of a kingdom of his own? "My kingdom," he had said. The words still echoed clearly in the minds of many.

It had now become clear to all that the kingdom of which Jesus had spoken was not Israel. That expectation was no longer a valid one. "My kingdom is not of this world." His words now stood forth with a significance not understood before. He is the king of a higher kingdom, a kingdom greater than Israel! Now dead and living beyond death, he would rule over a realm undying!

A play-yard filled with children suddenly surprised by an unparalleled happiness was never more exercised with exuberance than was now the company of disciples in and about the room.

The excitement grew as many things Jesus had said began to take on broader and deeper meanings. Philip and Nathanael began to write on their parchment, as one after another, and in groups of twos and threes, the disciples came forward with their contributions to an ever-increasing total.

So was the day spent until about the eleventh hour. Near this time I observed Matthew, Mathias, and Joseph Barsabas in prolonged conversation together. That this should be so was in no way unusual, but there was on this occasion an extraordinary earnestness in the way the three men spoke with one another. While not an argument, their discussion was exceptionally animated, and there was clearly a notable intensity about it.

Presently the three summoned six or seven others to join them, these including James, John, and Peter. There followed an exchange of thought most remarkable in depth and dimension, and so very compelling that virtually all the company were at length drawn into it.

Hesitatingly, apologetically, Joseph Barsabas opened the conversation specifically addressing Peter and the sons of Zebedee. He said, "We find ourselves deeply distressed. We have come to a dark place, nor can we lay hold of a torch to light our way out."

As he spoke, the distress with which he spoke also apparent in his voice, the anxiety of Matthew and Matthias became quickly mirrored in the faces of all who stood by. What unseemly intruder had now come to disturb the community?

"Go on," said Simon.

Barsabas continued uncertainly: "We are disciples, devoted to him we follow, believing him superior to all who live or ever lived. On this day, however, as we have walked in memory with the Master, we have blundered into something by which we are gravely troubled. We have discovered in him a strangeness that causes us to wonder."

A thick and dark apprehension settled like a cloud over the company.

"Go on," said Simon Peter again.

As Barsabas hesitated, Matthew spoke: "Contemplating the things Jesus said, we are shocked by a sudden awareness of certain things he did not say. We are perplexed by this. There were, apparently, strange silences and great open spaces in his teaching, and we cannot understand why. Many of the essential things a religious teacher would normally emphasize were things that apparently Jesus never mentioned at all."

"What things?" asked Peter.

Matthew answered, "Did any among us ever hear Jesus say that he believed in God?"

As Matthew paused uncertainly, a perplexity trembled its way through the assembly, a perplexity mingled with anxiety.

But the apostle went on: "A belief in God, to profess a belief in God — is not this virtually the first requirement of all teachers of religion? For that matter, did any among us ever hear Jesus say that he believed in anything? We assumed him a believer, yes. But did Jesus ever bear witness to any beliefs at all? Can any remember the words 'I believe' ever passed his lips?"

In response, waves of varied emotion swept through the assembly. There was consternation that the question should have arisen. There was anxiety as to why it had. And there was amazement that it might possibly suggest a truth.

Within moments, though, as emotions subsided, it was generally acknowledged that Jesus had never been heard to profess a personal belief in God. Strange, very strange, and the realization fell heavily upon the company. Yes, Jesus had spoken often of God, usually as "my Father," always assuming existence, but never confessing faith. Strange, very strange. And strange, too, the way a company of learners, honestly listening, might have overlooked so much for so long.

This troubling question was only the first of several. Immediately came a second, offered by Barsabas, as I remember: "Did Jesus ever speak of anything God had ever done for him, any mercy shown, any blessing given?"

Surely such a witness would be expected of any person seeking to lead others toward God. None were able to recall that Jesus had ever spoken of God at all in this way, and most were startled to discover it so.

Then further disturbing waters already troubled, Matthias

put forth a third question: "Was Jesus ever known to confess any sin or sinfulness or to seek for himself the forgiveness of God?" What of Jesus, then, with respect to a normal humility in the presence of the Divine?

Disturbing as were these thoughts, they began to generate others. Among the company there were those who now commenced to ask questions of their own: "Were any able to remember that Jesus had ever testified to anything that a belief in God had done for him or meant to him?"

"Had Jesus ever acknowledged a personal debt of gratitude for God's mercy or forgiveness granted to him?"

Among many of the assembled disciples all this appeared as unsettling evidence of a faulty relationship with the Divine One. This beloved teacher — what sort of man was he, after all? The anxiety of the three had now overspread the assembly. It seemed that a dark pall overhung the room.

Into this came again the voice of Matthew, saying: "There is at least one question more. It is this: Did Jesus ever indicate, as religious leaders normally do, that God had called him apart for a sacred task, as he had, for example, Isaiah or Jeremiah or Amos or even Abraham or David?"

Moments of uneasy stillness followed, the silence then broken abruptly by a joyous outcry: "Oh, I see it now! Praise God, I see it!"

The voice was that of Matthew, responding to his own question. Astounded, the whole company turned to him, several saying, "What do you mean? What is it, Matthew?"

The usually staid and docile apostle was in high excitement now. He spoke with great fervor: "Oh, my friends, all the troubling questions have suddenly translated for me into a single glorious answer! And with what joy we can welcome it!"

One moment a disturbing question, the next a joyous answer — by what miracle could this come about? It was dumbfounding. What was this that had so forcibly struck the mind of Matthew? Instantly, though, John's face was illuminated by a full smile. Still smiling broadly, he turned to Matthew and said, "Tell us about it, good friend." Then, arms folded across his chest, John stood by in happy anticipation of Matthew's reply.

More calmly now and in the deliberate manner that was his usual way, Matthew responded: "It is true — Jesus made no claim that God had called him out from among the rest of us. But now consider this: He often declared that his Father had sent him to us! Not called from among us, but sent to us — here is the key. Understand this, and the great silences of Jesus no longer mystify. They are explained, they belong, they are essential actually. Do you perceive it? Jesus does not manifest a typically human approach to God or a typical relationship with God because he is not typically human! He is somewhat more, perhaps much, much more."

In a burst of exuberance, John rushed upon Matthew and embraced him. As he did so Simon Peter spoke, addressing all: "Surely we owe thanks to our three brothers. They have assisted us to think, and out of thought comes insight. I feel that they have brought us to the borderline of something great."

By now the attention of the entire assembly had come to focus on the issues raised by the three. Philip and Nathanael had left their writing and joined the others. As Peter concluded his comment, Philip, standing beside him, looked entreatingly up to the big man and said, "Forgive me, Simon, please forgive me, but I believe there is more that ought to be said."

"Go on, Philip," Peter replied. "Please proceed."

On this occasion the room was host to as many disciples as ever in the ten days, except the tenth. In order to be heard and seen, the diminutive Philip stood atop a chair and addressed the company: "Our three brothers have brought our attention to things Jesus never said, but that we, were we teachers, surely should and would. Please allow me now to turn this around and now to name certain things Jesus did say that you and I never could. As I think of it now, there are many of these. For example, who among us, issue of a woman's womb, would declare, 'The heavenly Father sent me,' and did we not at various times hear this from him? I remember also his saying, 'Come to me and I will give you rest.' Who among us would dare make that promise to anyone? I am sure too that, as did I, many of you heard him sometimes identify himself as 'the truth' or 'the bread of life.'

"There can be no doubt of it: Were any ever to say any of this, we would be rightfully regarded as impossibly demented or unforgivably vain. We have all this and more from Jesus; yet we respect and trust him.

"So, we have from Jesus his uncommon silences and his uncommon utterances — omission of the normally essential and inclusion of the normally impossible. Do not both bear witness to a single overwhelming truth? What is this truth, do you think?"

With this question, Philip gazed searchingly about the room and then stepped down from the chair. Silence followed.

It was Thomas who broke gently into it, saying, "Our brothers have said startling things. And I stand amazed that we could have been so long unaware of something so clearly apparent."

After a brief pause, and digressing somewhat, Thomas continued: "I suppose it a common fault of humankind: We often allow our assumptions to stand as walls around us, and if a meaning has any subtlety about it, it is likely distorted or destroyed when it tries to pass them. We often hear only what we assume we will. So do we add to what is not said and subtract from what is. We assumed Jesus a rabbi and so we heard him."

"Who is he then?" Carrying a tinge of impatience with it

the question came, I believe from Jerusalem's esteemed coppersmith. Then, amplifying his question, he added, "I know only two kinds of persons, the human and the divine."

It was James son of Zebedee who next spoke, his comment in part a response to the coppersmith. He spoke musingly, as though expressing a thought that had just come to mind: "We spoke of him sometimes as the Son of God. This we did as a compliment. We offered it as a conferred title of respect, I suppose, as any of us might honor another as 'child of Abraham' or 'son of David.' As it comes to me now, though, I suspect we were saying more than we knew."

From the room's farthest corner came a voice, a woman's voice, a voice I did not then identify, nor have I since: "If there is person human and if there is person divine, on which side stands he?"

"The thought overwhelms," said one.

"Is it possible?" said another, incredulously. "Is it possible that he may be...?"

As this voice dwindled into awed silence, another, that of Simon Peter, arose in its place: "Is it possible that he may be... not merely man, but... God? This is the question, is it not?"

"Not a question, but a certainty I think." It was John who said this. Then he went on: "Only if he were divine may certain silences and utterances of Jesus ever be understood or explained. Forgive my putting it this way, but we cannot make sense of Jesus except we see him as being divine."

The aged Benhabara, unable to be present most days because of infirmity, was nevertheless present on this day. Vigorous in mind and given to profound insight, this venerable Judean was adored as a father among disciples. From his place at the table he now lifted a frail arm, gesturing that those nearby come closer. As a good number did so, the aged one's voice arose with as much vigor as waning strength would allow. This was the only occasion on which

I ever heard Benhabara speak at any length, and memorable moments these were.

Tremorously and speaking slowly, the revered patriarch offered an insight none would ever forget. He said, "In future time I shall not have opportunity to offer much to this discipleship. Just now, though, I ask that you accept a small gift from me. I wish to give you something to think about.

"Actually, I suppose that what I wish to give you is a question. I hope you can hear it well and hereafter keep it ever before you. As between the human on the one hand and the divine on the other, with which did Jesus identify himself as a person? In all his dealings with us, which way was it?

"We have all long known that it was the purpose of Jesus to bring us closer to God. But in what way did he go about this? In what mode or manner did Jesus appeal to us? Was it a matter of 'you-and-I-reaching-up-to-God' or was it a matter of 'my-Father-and-I-coming-through-to-you'? Answer this and you have answered all."

His strength ebbing, the old man faltered. Then gathering all his remaining strength, he smiled slightly and added, "Thank you for hearing me."

Within a fortnight afterward the aged disciple was dead — gone, I think, to follow even more joyously the Leader he loved.

In my own time, now more than half a century later, his fellow-disciples are yet pondering that profound word spoken by a dying man. As for the immediate consequence, it was dynamic.

"Can it be? Can it possibly be?" someone somewhere mused aloud. "Can it be that in truth God has trudged in human sandals the rock-strewn hills of Galilee and Judea?"

Then another voice: "Is it possible that we walked with him and talked with him and never knew that he was he?"

Struck with awe at the very thought, many of the company fell to their knees and others variously expressed emotions as deep as human feelings ever run. A hush fell upon all.

Shortly after, the voice of John slowly ascended from the silence: "Let earth and heaven bear me witness now: With all my mind, with all my heart, with all that I am, I hold it true — in the coming of Christ, God has come."

"Yes, surely, but tell me this: When God comes, what next?" It was Thomas who said this and the question generated a thousand thoughts, these intermixed with a strange aura of anxiety and awe.

Before they were extinguished, the lamps that night required oil more than the normal number of times. The day had been a day of depth and stretched now to more than usual length. With minds overstressed and spirits in turbulence, it was as in a daze that most of the disciples found their ways to their places when at last they dispersed for the night.

As they were going, I saw Thomas look up to Peter as they walked, and I saw him lightly lay a hand on the big man's shoulder. The two paused, turned face to face, and Thomas said, "Simon, my friend, I have this thought: We think we are now discovering new things about Jesus; but you know, I believe that all the while he was trying to tell us of them, but we did not hear him."

In tones low and thoughtful, Peter replied, "Yes, Thomas, yes," and the two men walked away with the others.

VIII

The following day began slowly. Although the morning was clear and beautiful and the sun came up brilliantly from beyond the Kidron, many of the disciples were a long while arriving at the room. No doubt many were weary, physically fatigued from long days and lack of rest. Perhaps some suffered from the overwhelming emotional and mental travail of these last awesome days. Surely also there were those who deeply felt a need for solitude.

One of these was Matthew. It was at about the fifth hour that he came. Enjoying the warmth of springtime sun, there were by this hour a good number gathered on the terrace. As Matthew approached and was greeted, he expressed regret for having arrived late, then unpretentiously explained: "How very greatly I appreciate being together with all of you in this discipleship. My years at Capernaum's custom house were lonely ones. Jesus called me away from that and into this. I shall ever be thankful to him. Great is the privilege of being a follower of our Lord. But I want you to know this: The blessing is made infinitely greater because of you with whom I journey on the way.

"Forgive me please, but much as I appreciate all of you, today for a while I needed to be alone. From the governor's judgment hall, I walked the streets that go to Golgotha. Mostly I returned by the city wall. I needed to step aside and live for a while at the deepest level of myself. After the rapid pace of the recent past, I felt a need to pause and communicate with my soul. I needed to think."

As Matthew had spoken, a flood of love and good will was felt as it overflowed the company. But now as he concluded, and before any other had opportunity to speak, an abrasive voice broke harshly into the reverie: "You should think; there is much for you to think about."

It was the Zealot again; and his outburst precipitated a chill, a paralyzing effect upon everyone. Apparently this ardent patriot had long carried about with him a seething resentment of Matthew. A thoroughgoing foe of Rome, the Zealot had long harbored profound hostility toward his fellow disciple for his having formerly served the Romans. For nearly three years he had from time to time vainly attempted to make an issue of the matter.

During recent days, however, the Zealot had deepened and matured enormously in spirit, and it was assumed by most that he had overcome his deep-felt animosity. Now, abruptly and clearly apparent, there it was, and in the full force of its devastating power. The shock fell heavily upon the company, and for long, difficult moments all were speechless. After all, what could be said?

Shocked as they were by what had just happened, the company was equally startled by what happened next. First to speak was the Zealot himself, again. All the harshness now gone from his voice, there was only a pathos, a plaintive contrition: "Oh, my friends, what have I done! Some ugly thing has spoken from within me. Forgive me, my brother! Forgive me, everyone! Rome does not matter anymore. It is only this discipleship that matters to me now. I am sorry, so sorry."

Great tears can well instantly in the eyes of a troubled child, but normally not so freely in eyes that are older. However, before he finished speaking the Zealot's tears were falling already upon the pavement at his feet.

Some of those present ran to the Zealot, others rushed to the side of Matthew. Within moments, though, the two clusters were intermingled, and at the center Matthew and the Zealot, together in strong embrace, commingled tears of reconciliation and peace.

Never was it known afterward that the Zealot felt anything other than love and good will for anyone. While he continued always to hold Rome in the wrong, he saw every Roman as a fellow human and beloved of God equally with all others.

The zeal that had been his for the kingdom of Israel died away and rose again as an all-encompassing passion for the kingdom of our Lord Jesus Christ. This, in all his remaining years, the Zealot served well. He and Matthew drew close in friendship, very close, and remained so until the very day the Zealot died.

It is now fourteen years since his death, and the memory of this man remains fresh and fragrant amongst us. He was one of many who have died for the Faith. Although he had long before made his peace with Romans, it was they who took his life at last. Nero's Roman minions seized him at Scorda, and it is said that as they were preparing his execution he prayed for them, repeating a prayer his Lord once offered: "Father, forgive them."

On the terrace on this pleasant morning, the Zealot's bitter invective actually worked for good among the disciples. One consequence, of course, was the final resolution of the issue between the two apostles.

Another was the introduction of a thought that would at length emerge as a primary tenet of our Faith. This developed from the before-and-after contrast in the life of Matthew and was precipitated as Simon Peter remarked, "Becoming a disciple, whatever one has been is past; somehow, entering this discipleship is like beginning again."

There followed some speculation concerning this and no small amount of rejoicing. Even greater, though, would have been the joy could those who talked of this have known of a small drama being at that very moment played out on a Jerusalem street.

First word of this came with the coming of Seth the Hebronite and the devoted Bartimaeus, whom Seth had brought up from Jericho and assisted in many ways. Seth was Hebron's innkeeper, widely known in the area, a genteel and generous citizen. His discipleship dated from the previous year, and among the disciples he occupied a place of high esteem. He was one of many faithful followers who had not traveled much with Jesus, but whose loyalty was equally as strong as that of any who had.

As the Hebronite and his companion now joined the assembled company, it was apparent to all that an aura of joy was about them. Immediately behind them, ascending the stair, were two men — newcomers and strangers. One was aged, older than the other by almost forty years, as was later learned. The old man carried in one hand a shepherd's staff and with the other clutched firmly the arm of the younger.

Reaching the terrace first, the two disciples turned and silently waited as the others came.

Seth then addressed the company: "These men we met today on a street nearby, and there for a long while we talked together. They are Etham and his son Raymel, shepherds from the hill country east of Betzin. This father and son have traveled on a diligent quest, and it may be that today they have found what they seek. I feel that Etham has a thing of much importance to say to us. Is it acceptable that we hear him?"

Seth's request heartily approved, a chair was brought, and with the aid of his son, the old man lowered himself into it. Raymel stood at his father's shoulder. Disciples gathered about.

The old man's wizened small frame somehow seemed out of keeping with his poise and the cultivated manner of his speech. Though the voice was feeble from age, the eyes projected a vitality that normally belongs only to the young.

Commencing with a warming smile and a level glance about him, the aged one said, "Raymel and I thank you for this hospitality and for the opportunity of speaking with you.

We are especially thankful for the graciousness of Seth and Bartimaeus in bringing us to you.

"Lifelong, I have been a keeper of sheep, as has also my son. It is now more than thirty years since we watched our flock on a certain winter night not far from the old City of David. All these years I have pondered a thing that happened there. And lately I have had cause to marvel even more. It is for this reason that we have come to you.

"I must speak of that night. All was quiet, the air still, the stars clear, the flock at rest. My son and I — he was a mere lad then — sat huddled together against the nighttime chill. Suddenly we felt a presence, although there was no sound and the flock never stirred. Our dog, half sleeping at my feet, aroused and looked about but did not bark. We sat very still, the two of us, listening.

"Then we heard a sound, or thought we did, a subtle cadence like music, so it seemed. At first I thought it perhaps a sudden stirring of wind on a distant hill. But no, it was nearer than this, seeming to arise all around and to float down as from above. As we listened intently, trying to understand the mystery of this, there presently came a voice, coming not from near us, but from somewhere beyond — we heard it clearly.

"Looking upward, we saw a star, or what at first we thought a star, a star much brighter than others, and as we watched we saw it grow and draw near, and the form of it changed, and the voice grew clear, the words in the Aramaic tongue, but rising and falling in the modulations and crescendos of great music.

"That which we saw and heard that night caused us to leave the flock and run to the city and seek the inn that was there. Here we found a newborn child, as the voice had said we would.

"All my remaining years I have wondered about that child — that infant boy. Especially in these later years, I have wondered what has become of him, and even more recently now, my son and I have gone forth trying to find out.

"We learned of your Jesus and of all that has transpired in these last weeks. The age would be about right. And numerous other discoveries have led us to believe that this Jesus was that child.

"For a long while I have known of this good man Seth, a man from our country, a man of compassion and integrity. Then, not long since, we learned that Seth was of this discipleship, a follower of this Jesus. Thus we sought him and so he has brought us to you.

"Raymel and I must know if indeed Jesus is that child. I must know. Something within me requires my knowing. Tell me, friends, tell me, what do you think? Is he or is he not?"

Here the aged one ended his speech, awaiting an answer, again surveying the faces about him, but this time in more solemn mien.

It was Simon Peter who replied: "We welcome your coming, Etham and Raymel. We welcome your word, Etham. In answer to your question, I can tell you this: We have long known that Jesus was born at Bethlehem."

His eyes aglow, a smile touched the old man's lips, and he nodded as though pleased with what he heard.

From the edge of the assembly near the stair came a woman's voice, tremulous with feeling: "May I pass, please?"

The crowd parted, a path opened, and the mother of John and James moved forward to stand before the hill-country shepherd. She said, "I am Salome, sister of Jesus' mother. Do you know the time, Etham — the month, the day?"

"That or this?" the old man asked.

"That," Salome answered, "that, the date of the night when you found the child."

"Yes, I know it," replied Etham, "I have not forgotten. I remember it well. It was the night of the 21st day of the month of Tebeth."

"That," answered Salome evenly, "that was the date of his birth. Jesus was indeed born on the 21st day of the month of Tebeth! My sister has often told me of it."

A visible tide of joy enveloped the two shepherds and then seemed to overflow all who stood by. "Then it is true, it is true, as I deeply felt it was. The child I looked upon that night is the Jesus you have followed this while." Etham's voice trembled, the emotion of the moment engulfing him.

Calmly then, and in reflective mood, the shepherd continued: "You know, Raymel and I may have been his first disciples. They who seek also follow, do they not? Perhaps it is from afar they follow, but they are followers nonetheless.

"While I never knew his name or who he really was, that child has possessed me all these years. And as the years accumulated to great number, the greater became my passion to find him. I have found him now, and I am content."

Rarely does human feeling run deeper than it ran at Jotham's house just then, and probably there were as many feelings as persons present. For most, though, feelings deeper still were yet to be stirred as Etham continued.

He said, "My dear good people, I feel a kinship with you. We are disciples of the same Lord, and I think that perhaps I was before you were. I nearly envy you the privilege that has been yours these last years. How good it must have been to have walked with him! I join you now and from here we walk together.

"On this day you have greatly blessed me. Now I wish to say a thing that may bless you. There is this we wish you to know, and I believe you will be blessed in the knowing. Raymel and I believe he was a heavenly messenger who spoke with us near Bethlehem that night. Whoever he was who spoke, the message was an identifying one. The message told us who the infant was. No, not by name; we never knew that. It was in a far more significant way that we knew him and have known him all these years. Out from the cadences of that night, one word came clear and clearly lingers still: Today to you is a Savior born.

"Savior!" As with a single breath the word burst from many throats.

"May this be the word?" shouted someone, James I think. "Is this the defining word that tells us who he is?"

Almost instantly, all speaking at once, the disciples were swept into commotion as by a storm. All knew, I think, that they had come to a landmark point in their journey, although no doubt some did not fully comprehend how or why.

The disciples had long seen Jesus as a person of importance and authority, and so had spoken of him as Lord. Now, in these last days they had concluded him to be the Messiah, the Anointed One, the Christ. They had now come to understand him as having been sent to them, rather than arising from among them.

But the meaning continued to elude them. What relevance had all this for them and for any others? Now dead and risen, in what way, if any, did Jesus relate to the world of living, struggling, and searching humanity?

"Savior," the aged shepherd had said. Or was it an angel who said that? Savior! Could there be a greater need on earth? Savior! What role greater than this may anyone ever play in the drama of life? May it be that now, quite instantaneously, we know who Jesus really is? With such thoughts, the excitement was great on the terrace in that hour.

As the furor subsided somewhat, the aged shepherd's presence almost forgotten now, the company fell into serious consideration of the message he had brought. In general tenor the discussion went this way: "Over our long history we have sought salvation, to be absolved of sin's guilt. This has been a primary concern in Israel, as also in the rest of the world, apparently. We have devised intricate schemes to rid ourselves of guilt, and so to come near to God.

"We have undertaken to transfer our sins to animals and

send them away into the wilderness to perish. We have laid hands on bulls and lambs and then slain them, hoping our sins were annihilated when these animals died. We have offered sacrifice of our substance, hoping to appease the God against whom we had sinned.

"As one of our prophets said, we have offered the fruits of our bodies for the sins of our souls. So we have desperately sought to do the things that might save us.

"But long ago our prophets proclaimed it all in vain, of no avail. And deeply, we have known it so. Nothing we might do could undo the evil we had done; all we could hope was that God might forgive. But why should he? We tried purchasing mercy from God, buying into his generosity. But no action of ours could do that.

"Now it is God who has acted. He has done what we never could do: He has sent one to us, and in that one he himself has come. We know this now. In these last days we have discovered it true.

"He is Messiah. We had long assumed he would set us free from those who oppress us; we now know that Rome yet rules. Comes he then not to set us free from our enemies, but from ourselves, from the sins that enslave us?

"We tried our sacrifices; now God has offered his. We here at this place have lately pondered the mystery of Jesus. Realizing that they did not take his life but that he gave it, we have questioned why. Now we know.

"May it be that all this past system of sacrificing was but a poor image of the ultimate? No longer shall a sinner lay his hand on the head of a goat and slay it, for God has offered one sacrifice for all Israel and perhaps for all the world. Not on account of bulls or goats or lambs offered in sacrifice, but for the sake of him who offered himself, God offers forgiveness of sin.

"Who is Jesus, then? He is Savior! Bit by bit, the mystery surrenders to the light. He is our Lord, Jesus the Christ,

Savior. And who are we, his disciples? We are they who must make it known. All Israel must be told, and beyond Israel, the world."

I think it was at this time, on this day, on the rooftop of Jotham's house, that the laborious quest for identity was most significantly rewarded. Here the disciples made the one discovery that, more than any other, put them on the course that until our present time they have firmly held.

Suddenly the death over which they had grieved became for them a supreme act of divine love. Suddenly they understood that the post-resurrection life would be the divine channel through which salvation would forever flow. Suddenly for them the death was no longer a tragedy nor the resurrection a pointless mystery. Suddenly they saw that great purpose was here. And great joy overflowed them on Jotham's terrace that day.

Well, late in the day came the time when the messengers from Bethlehem would go their way. Near exhaustion now, the aged shepherd announced that they must leave. As Raymel helped him from the chair, there were those who graciously spoke to the younger man, who smiled but made no reply. Etham lifted a hand, gesturing silence, glanced approvingly toward his son, and quietly said, "My son has never spoken; he cannot speak."

Immediate expressions of sympathy and regret came from all about, these, though, to be quickly silenced as Ethan again raised a hand, saying as he did so, "As my son's father, I have much to be thankful for; while he cannot speak, his heart is great with love."

So saying, the old man turned as with a blessing to the younger, and with this the younger man swept the frail figure of the old one into his arms and lightly carried him down the stair and away.

Thomas turned to James and I heard him say, "If Ashabel or Marcus Gracian should ask their great question now, we could answer them, don't you think?"

"Praise God, yes," James replied, and the two locked arms and walked into the room.

IX

Joseph of Arimathea had been several days in Joppa, there to care for a shipment of merchandise coming in from across the Great Sea. He had only yesterday returned to his home in Jerusalem, and today he was one of the first to arrive at the room.

As disciples gradually gathered he spoke amicably with those who came, and when a sizable congregation had assembled he said, "My wife and Mary intend to come later today. I come early, for I have urgent need to speak with you."

Most of the disciples were not often in the company of the rich and powerful, and I believe that some felt some discomfort in these moments. Arimathea, though, was a modest and ordinary sort of man, blessed with a genuine liking for people, a quality that encouraged others to be at ease in his presence. Soon today, therefore, the mood about the room was altogether as usual.

Nevertheless, it was Joseph of Arimathea to whom most gave their attention. That attention soared sharply as the man said, "There is something that troubles me greatly, and I think you may be able to help me with it."

After only an instant's hesitation, Simon Peter replied, "If you are troubled, brother Joseph, then we are distressed with you."

With apparent sincerity, but without visible emotion, Joseph continued, "Actually, it is an unanswered question that I am bothered by. The question has plagued me severely since the day Jesus died. You know that it was I who went to the governor and obtained permission to entomb the body of Jesus. It troubles me that I had not gone to Pilate sooner. Had I done so, perhaps I may have forestalled the execution.

What do you think?"

There was a long silence but not an inactive one. It was an interlude in which virtually every person earnestly reached out in spirit to this good man, in the anxiety that was heavy upon him. At last it was James who answered him: "No one can know what the governor might have done. But please, Joseph, let it not trouble you. Whatever he may have done would probably not have mattered greatly."

Quickly and with a voice expressing surprise, Joseph said, "What are you saying? I do not understand. The governor's decision would not have mattered?"

James and Simon Peter exchanged glances, James nodded, and Peter spoke: "Brother Joseph, we have made startling discoveries in this place in these days. In the new light of these last weeks, we have been able to see our Lord Jesus as we had not seen him before. Now that he has died and is risen, much that he did and said beforehand is seen to have meanings we never knew were there. Now that we better understand who he was and is, I think we can tell you this: Whatever the governor may have decided, it was inevitable that Jesus would suffer, and probably to the point of dying."

Aghast, Joseph responded, "How can you say this, Simon? How can you know?"

Peter replied evenly, "When the love of our good and holy God meets the sins of earthlings, there will be pain."

"I fail to understand your meaning, Simon. What are you saying to me?"

"I am saying," said Peter, "that Jesus was not one of us, a sinner searching for forgiveness and for God, but that he was himself the divine being come to us in our own flesh and form."

"What!" Joseph called out in astonishment, "May it possibly be?"

"Yes," replied Peter calmly, "so it may be, and so, we are convinced, it is. He came to us to save us from our sins. And sin never tolerates interference graciously. He was bound to suffer, and he knew it, and he was willing."

As Joseph stood in thoughtful silence, Peter turned to James, and it was James then who picked up and carried forward Peter's thought: "You see, Joseph, it was not the governor who took the life of Jesus, nor was it even the soldiers, not really. Jesus *gave* his life. Jesus himself had spoken of it: There at Pilate's judgment hall or at Mount Golgotha, Jesus might have called legions of angels to his rescue. And what a scattering of swords and phylacteries only one angel might have wrought in either place that day! By a single uplifted finger, soldiers and priests could have been sent flying. But did Jesus summon his angels? No. If we must say that the enemies of Jesus took his life, then let us quickly add that they were able to do so only because he allowed them."

"I remain confused," Joseph said. "You say it was inevitable Jesus would suffer?"

It was John who responded: "Perhaps it is needful that this be explained a little. You see, sir, in all he did all along the way, Jesus was coming to us, trying to get through to us. We saw this in all his teaching and in every act. But we never understood until now how far he meant to come.

"Where are we of this humanity? We are in our sins. It was the greatest of the prophets who said, 'God's hand is not shortened that he cannot save.' Our God has a long reach. But the prophet also said, 'Your sins have separated between you and your God.' So there is this barrier. And if our Lord Christ is to get through to us, he could not bypass that. To confront it would be painful; he knew this, and he was willing.

"Yes, he might have shunned the pain. He might have drawn back and avoided it. Suppose he had? Then he would have stopped short of coming all the way to us, wouldn't he? Having already come so far — initially from heaven we think, and on earth from Bethlehem — he would not turn aside when he came to his journey's painful part.

"From the beginning, in the whole of his journey, he was on course for the ultimate encounter. And at his cross he came up head-on against that awful barrier that has so long separated creature from Creator. And holiness could not, without distress, confront this ugly thing.

"Hence the suffering, sir. Hence the cross. Hence the dying. But the barrier is broken. The separating wall is breached. Henceforth, all who will may pass."

John ceased. Held in the power of what he had said, no one spoke and no one moved. After a few moments of immobility, John spoke again, now in a tone of apology: "Forgive me, sir, but if I may, I will go on to say yet another thing, and this we think of great importance. The death we assumed the end of things appears now to have been a new beginning. And it appears, too, that Jesus intended it to be. And this we know: By his resurrection Jesus lives — forever, we are sure. And, of course, there is no resurrection without first a death.

"Thus, Jesus used his death as an instrument of high purpose. He made of it a way of coming closer to us and of being everlastingly with us. Death, having laid hands on him once, can never touch him again. He has overcome it, he has gone beyond it, and he has used it to overcome the limitations of body. Now free in the realm of spirit, he uses this freedom to come to us, to be with us, and to deliver to us the forgiveness and redeeming mercy of God. His death, you see, sir, has become a door of entrance that we are certain will never close."

Entranced, Joseph had listened with full attention to all that John had said, a mingling of amazement and incredulity visible in his countenance. Now, with the focus of one accustomed to penetrating the heart of matters, he asked, "Are you saying, young man, that the death of Jesus was a good thing?"

"Ultimately, yes." It was James who answered, and then he went on: "Not good in itself, no, but in its consequences. And the consequences — what are these? Chief among them — salvation. We are confident of this: Jesus is Savior. Henceforth, it is not by reason of slain beasts, but by reason of one who loved unto death that our sins will be forgiven. We firmly hold it true: Our Lord Jesus is Messiah, is Savior. In him, God has moved to touch the world as the world has never been touched before."

Thoughtfully, Joseph replied: "I am thankful for your answer to my question. I have received more than I asked. I doubt that I fully understand, but now that you have told me more about Jesus, his death does not trouble me so much. But it moves me more. And I feel that in course of time it will move me more deeply yet."

Appearing to have said all he intended, Joseph paused, then immediately spoke again: "Now I leave you with this: The tomb in which the body of Jesus once laid — I am resolved that never in all time shall any other be laid in it. I wish you to know this. Although the tomb was made for me, I am unworthy of it now."

Joseph turned, moved three or four paces toward the door, and then hesitated. Looking about he located the young apostle who normally identified himself as the one Jesus loved. Stepping over to him, Joseph asked, "What is your name, young man?"

Surprised and somewhat startled by the question, the young apostle politely replied, "My name is John, sir, brother of James and son of Salome and our late father Zebedee."

"I shall remember," replied Joseph, "and I shall expect to hear of you again."

Moving to the doorway, Joseph stopped there, turned, lifted a hand as in benediction, saying, "I salute you, dear friends, and I thank you. Pray for my peace; I shall pray for yours."

The good man had not yet reached the street when the peace for which he would pray was gravely disturbed. From between clenched teeth came a cynical whisper, directed no doubt to the hearing of one or two but oozing gall and heard by many.

It was from the enigmatic Jonas Ben Eban that the whisper came, and the words were these: " 'I shall expect to hear of you again'? I am weary of it; I detest that boy and all who applaud him!"

Standing alongside Ben Eban, and apparently his intended audience or a substantial part of it, was the much younger man, Micah son of Urial. All who heard instantly turned, the two men finding themselves immediately surrounded by a circle of troubled faces.

"Well, say something, one of you," growled Ben Eban when after a long while no person had spoken or moved. Following this defiant exclamation, still no one moved or spoke, all maintaining a circle of silence, gazing in piteously upon the two at the center.

"You may as well know," shouted Ben Eban at last, "I am sick of the threesome who manage this charade, especially the young one." Still no one spoke. Ben Eban hesitated uncertainly, tentatively, and then in a manner more subdued, he said, "You expect me to apologize, but I will not." Two or three reached out to him, but he pushed them away. Then in a sudden flash of defiance he virtually snarled, "I am going, and once I pass that threshold," waving toward the doorway, "I will never cross it again. Are you coming with me, Micah?" As Ben Eban elbowed his way to the exit, Micah hesitated a little and then followed.

While Ben Eban, a rather reclusive fellow, had come late into the company, and little was known of his past activities or present attitudes, his leaving and the manner of it, was a matter of much distress for those around him. Especially grievous was the man's apparent influence on the youthful and more genteel Micah.

As the two men departed, tears that welled in the eyes of Simon Peter overflowed and ran in streamlets down his ruddy face. Various others were equally affected. When the company was able to compose itself, the first concern was to provide comfort and reassurance to Simon Peter and James and especially John.

Afterward, Simon Peter spoke to the assembly: "We must pray for these who have gone away. What shall we ask for them?"

Answers came from here and there throughout the room, these generally reflecting laudable insight, charity, and compassion on the part of those who offered them. Then, a meaningful roster of petitions having been named, the disciples gave themselves to prayer for a time.

Following the final "amen," Nathanael spoke: "We have given much attention to two matters: first, the meaning of Jesus' death, and second, the many things he said. I feel that both considerations are of enormous importance to us. As the two of these now come together in my mind, a question emerges specifically on the occasion of his death: what did Jesus say?"

Going on then to explain his question, Nathanael said, "Some were present when he died, but I was not. I have tried to imagine how it was. Lately I have been obsessed by the thought of it. I have inquired of some, and you have told me what you could. But the more I learn the more I long to know. There is a yearning within me to enter in, to feel the awesomeness of that time. This yearning I believe many feel. You who were witnesses to the events of that day, are you willing, for sake of us all, to live that time again and allow all of us to live it with you?"

Surprisingly, the first to respond was the gentle Joanna, and the nature of her response was likewise surprising, even shocking, and especially so coming from her. Standing a little apart with a small cluster of women, she separated herself from the group and turned to face Nathanael, her clear, calm voice rising above the usual sounds of rustling garments and sandals on flagstones.

She said: "Nathanael! You say you were not there the day Jesus died. Well, why?"

Obviously startled, Nathanael offered no immediate reply, and Joanna continued: "During these many weeks I have allowed a question to pester me. I have pretty well worked my way through it, and I supposed I would never mention the matter. But I will. Of all who followed Jesus, why were so few with him when he died? I believe six of us women were there, but of the apostles only John. I feel no bitterness about it, only perplexity. I hold no resentments against anyone. But it has troubled me that with this solitary exception, only a small group of women would go with him to the end."

Joanna asked no reply, no explanation. However, there were those present who offered comments nevertheless.

One: "I loved him and I thought I could not bear to see him die."

Another: "I confess that I was afraid. With the leader condemned, would the followers be next?"

Yet another: "I think I was numb from the anxiety of it all. The day I spent mostly in Gethsemane and wandering alone in the valley and the mount beyond."

Simon the Zealot: "I saw the cause as lost; to me, nothing mattered anymore. The thought, I fear, never came to mind of following him to his death. I was prepared to follow him alive to Jerusalem or to Rome, but not to a cross. Not then."

Simon Peter: "Burdened by my shame, I was a long while somewhere weeping. My tears at last all spent, I arose, took a deep breath, and set forth running. When I reached Mount Golgotha, I met the multitude coming down. I sat at the curbside, listened to their chatter as they passed, and wept again."

Hearing her companions speak in this manner, Joanna responded from within that marvelous spirit that was hers. Countenance aglow, she said: "Oh my precious ones, I love you all. I really and deeply do. We have come so long a way together. And surely we are more and more together as the days come and go. Increasingly, I feel of these days, not as a waiting time, but as a precious time of fellowship. Now, all of you please forgive me, and Nathanael, you especially. When I intruded with my foolish question, we were about to think of the happenings of our Lord's dying. Shall we get on with it?"

Joanna smiled on those about her, and most smiled in return. Always when Joanna bestowed the blessing of her smile, it was hard not to return it. And this instance was not an exception, this despite the serious character of that to which the company was about to give its attention.

At this moment, a flurry of motion near the doorway directed attention thither. The mother of Jesus and the wife of Arimathea came into the room.

After greetings, Simon Peter addressed Mary: "It is good to have you come. We know that you grieve for your lost son, and we would wish to relieve the grief and not to worsen it. Just now as you arrive, however, for sake of our understanding, we are about to review the circumstances of his death. This, if you prefer, we will forego for now."

Unhesitatingly, Mary replied, "It will not trouble me, Simon. I have relived it many times and no doubt will do so again and yet again, but no longer in throes of sorrow. I feel it deeply: Death has not taken my son from me; death has but released him into a larger life, and I am content to have it so. Somehow, strangely, my son is more than a son to me now. Speak of the crucifixion if you wish; I shall be at peace about it."

So saying, Mary moved to the table and was seated there, Marshia, Joanna, Salome, and others of the women joining her, Salome being seated alongside Mary at her left.

At the table, Salome was first to speak. Turning to Mary and placing a hand on hers, she said, "My beloved sister, you and I have a son in common now. It is the will of Jesus by word spoken from the cross as he died. Come, John."

She gestured and John approached, pausing to stand in the rear by the two of them. Momentarily both women turned to him, each clasping a hand.

Then Salome said, "Among the things I heard Jesus say when dying was an especially thoughtful and tender thing. Speaking from the cross and looking benignly down upon the seven of us tightly clustered there, he asked that Mary and John always look upon each other as mother and son. I desire all to know this: As John's mother and Mary's sister, I hope they always will."

Again, Salome placed her hand on Mary's and the sisters smiled each into the eyes of the other. John stood a pace back. It was a warm and happy moment.

Some of the disciples, I am sure, were surprised to learn that Jesus had committed his mother to John's care, and some no doubt wondered why he should have done so. It was, I think, a matter of family relationship. The ties of love between the two sisters in the one generation, and those among their three sons in the next, were close and of great satisfaction to all.

Mary's own stepchildren, however, had long manifested a casual and almost callous indifference to her. This had grieved Joseph deeply during his final years and had greatly worsened following his death. Then as Jesus had gone about his teaching career and the fame of him had spread abroad, there had developed among Joseph's children a resentment that further widened the breach.

Following the crucifixion, however, as I have earlier said, certain among Joseph's children, notably James, came to look favorably upon Jesus, some eventually becoming his disciples.

With regard to events of the day Jesus died, the disciples had no knowledge that Jesus had spoken at all between the time the cross was laid on him at the governor's judgment hall and the time they nailed him to it at the place of crucifixion. By the time of crucifixion, though, the six women and John were present, attending him there, observing every sign, and hearing every word.

About the great table in Jotham's upper room, memories of the crucifixion were freely shared, sometimes in high excitement, sometimes with deep feeling, and sometimes there were tears. Speaking from the cross that day, what were the things their dying Lord had said?

Salome had already mentioned one. Next named was this: "Father, forgive these men, for they do not know what they are doing." He who had taught forgiveness had proved himself forgiving. All present were deeply moved by the thought of this. Then came a thought equally moving: Clearly Jesus had been accurate in his saying; indeed, the crucifiers knew not what they did. Believing they crucified one, they actually crucified another, for Jesus was far more than they assumed him to be.

Mary of Magdala knew more than most the meaning of forgiveness in human life. She now told of a crucifixion episode that had moved her profoundly. It involved two criminals, thieves who were being crucified alongside Jesus. One of these loudly called out to our Lord, "If you are the Messiah, then deliver us from these crosses." Apparently the man wished to return again to his thieving. Jesus made no reply.

The other thief, looking forward, saw Jesus as moving forward to something better and he desired to go with him. This man said, "Please remember me when you have come into your kingdom." Instantly Jesus answered him, "I declare to you that before this day ends you will be with me in my realm."

Thus, three times, from the cross, Jesus had spoken, and

each time out of concern for others — his mother, his tormentors, and a dying thief.

Then afterward, with the pangs of death hard upon him, he had spoken out of his own agony. Once, in pained outcry, came forth words from an ancient psalm: "My God, why have you forsaken me?" Once he called for water, but they gave him none. Toward the end, he murmured "It is finished," and many have since pondered the meaning of this. At last, as in calm surrender, and speaking quite clearly now, he said, "My Father, into your hands I give my spirit."

Here in the room, among these several witnesses, these several speeches came to mind clearly and quickly, and were easily recited, and briefly discussed. Then suddenly there were no more; no one could think of any. It was as the abrupt closing of a door, and a long quiet settled in.

While he had carefully attended all that was said, John had not spoken. Now he spoke. Having the attention of all present, he said: "I have numbered them. The total is seven; we have here named seven utterances of Jesus spoken from the cross when he was dying. Were these all? Suddenly it comes to me: There was one other, the eighth. I cannot quote it for you. It was spoken in a language I did not fully understand, nor do I now. But it may have said more than any of us will ever know."

Struggling with powerful emotions John paused, the company immobile, almost breathlessly expectant. Regaining a measure of composure, John continued: "He cried with a loud voice. We who were there heard that. This was his final utterance, this his eighth word. It was, I suppose, an expression of the ultimate pain, the final sorrow. I cannot translate it into any language we know. I doubt if any can. For who is able to measure the full dimension of a cry, any cry, but especially that one?

"The time comes, though, for all of us I suppose, when there is no word but a cry. When all language is exhausted, when all the words have been used up, when all that can be said has been said, and then nothing is left but a cry.

"And I would guess that we all come to the eighth word at last. Whether spoken from a cross or a throne, the time comes at length when no language amenable to tongue or pen can say what must be said. It may be that a cry is the ultimate language of the soul. Other languages may express lesser meanings, but at length all tongues must fail.

"The content of a cry — who may know it? Only God perhaps. Perhaps, finally, every cry is addressed only to God and only God may understand it.

"And that cry which arose from the heart of Jesus and escaped his lips at Golgotha that day — who but God may know the meaning of that? In this world, many cries have passed many lips, and without doubt many yet will, but there never was, and I think will never be, another cry like that one."

There was evidence that John had not anticipated what he would say and that his thoughts were causal (each generating the next), and that they were as new to him as they were to those who heard him. When he left off speaking, it was as one who, stepping softly, has ventured so far into the whispering precincts of a holy temple that even the whispering must subside into silence.

Now, with no further word, and leaving a rapt audience in its place, John slowly walked to the doorway, crossed the terrace, and stood for a long while alone at the westward parapet silently gazing into the sunset.

X

The eighth day of the ten was the seventh day of the week, a sabbath. On this day there was more than the usual amount of coming and going as disciples moved in and out of the room. Virtually all visited nearby synagogues, some more than once.

It was at about the seventh hour when John and James returned from such a visit. From the moment the brothers came into the room, it was clear that powerful feelings possessed them. But the company were all attentive to Thomas, who was reading aloud from the prophet Hosea. As the two sons of Zebedee and Salome quietly took their places in the group, Thomas continued the reading: "Come, let us turn again to the Lord our God, for though we are torn, he will heal us, and though we are struck down, he will lift us up. After a day or two he will revive us, and on the third day he will raise us up, so that we may live in his care. Therefore, let us strive to know the Lord God; let us move speedily to know him well. For he will come to us; as surely as the next dawn, he will come; he will come like the winter rain, like springtime showers, watering the land."

As he completed the reading and placed the scroll on the table, Thomas said, "It is as though this message is for us at this precise time. And surely it is ever a comfort for all who stand in uncertain places. I suppose the more insecure our place, the greater should be our confidence in God. We gathered here are travelers on an unfamiliar road. We know not where it leads, how far we have come on it, nor how far we have yet to go.

"We disciples have followed one who led, and surely we would follow still. Oh, if only we might see him beckon or hear him call! I am sure that from our hearts we call out to him. Is he somewhere listening? Oh, that he might give us a sign, a signal that we might see and understand! So much like children are we, orphans lost and wandering. Oh, to hear a voice, to see a light! We wait, and waiting is hard to do. Waiting is a time for trusting, as for us of this discipleship all times must always be. Intervals are usually difficult. But it is the nature of intervals always to pass. And this will. Is it not so?"

Thomas had spoken slowly, reflectively expressing his thoughts as they came to him, following where they led, not knowing where that might be. All who heard attended carefully. But to the question with which he concluded there was no response.

Instead, near me someone said, "This is the eighth day."

At that moment from somewhere came notes of song, and after the first few words the singer was joined by most of the others present: "O Lord, our Lord, how majestic is your name in all the earth..." Then followed others of the songs and prayers of Israel.

At length James arose from his place, saying, "There is something my brother and I desire to speak with you about, something that struck us with great power today. It came to us at the synagogue, and I am not sure we know what to make of it. John speaks better than I and I would like him to speak with you of this."

John hesitated, making no move, saying nothing. Then responding to murmurs of encouragement, the younger brother of James arose and walked slowly to the place Thomas had stood, three or four scrolls lying on the table before him.

Glancing down momentarily at these, he then looked hesitantly about the room, apparently collecting his thoughts. Then he said, "Friends and fathers of this discipleship, I scarcely know how to say the thing I need to say now. I think it has never before been said, perhaps never even thought. We believe it of extreme importance, even essential to an understanding of who we are and the juncture to which we come."

All eyes were now turned to this earnest young man, some thirty pairs of them. John continued: "All of us have known from childhood that we of Israel have a unique place in the world, that we are a special people."

From somewhere came a voice, a voice with a hint of abrasion in it: "Do you doubt that we are?"

To this intrusion John did not immediately respond, and during a long pause there was throughout the room a total and apprehensive quiet.

At length John replied, "No, I do not doubt that we are. In fact, we may be more special than we have ever known. Our role in the human drama may prove other and greater than we have supposed or dreamed."

Picking up again the thread of his thought, John went on: "We of Israel have long seen ourselves as a chosen instrument of God. We have long believed that through us, as a people, God would one day perform a great wonder for humankind. When we have looked soberly upon it, we have seen ourselves, at our best, as a servant people, and we have been taught to expect suffering in our serving."

John spoke slowly, deliberately, his brother standing somewhat apart, observing and listening intently. With a glance toward him, John returned to his exposition: "Today at the synagogue, as the prophet was read, the reading spoke to my brother and me as it had never spoken before. The ancient and familiar words came to us with a message that was new and different. I suppose that new circumstances may throw new light on old truth. Nevertheless, listening, a sudden thought, wholly new to us, leaped at once into both our minds. Startled, I turned to James; he, with equal astonishment, turned to me. As our eyes met, each knew and understood the thought of the other. Allow me now to read from the prophet some of that which we heard today, and perhaps the thought that came to us may also come to you."

John lifted the Isaiah scroll from its place, rolled it forward a little, and began thoughtfully to read: "He was despised and rejected by men, a man of sorrows, and acquainted with grief."

Halting, but holding the scroll in his two hands, the young apostle turned earnestly to those about him, saying: "We have always believed this a reference to ourselves as a people, that it is we of Israel who are the despised and rejected, that ours are the sorrow and the grief. Have we not seen ourselves as the disfigured servant, looked on by others with disdain, but one day to be revealed as a great power in the world?"

John paused as though expecting an answer to his question, but there was none. With a glance toward the scroll he held, and indicating it with a gesture, he said, "All know this sacred scripture well, this passage especially. Once again, hear it now: 'He did no violence, and there was no deceit about him; yet he was despised and ill-esteemed; he was counted as a criminal.' Who is 'he'? Who is best described here?"

At this, a torrent of amazement overflowed the room. A one-word question came from somewhere in the midst: "Him?"

Striving to control a powerful emotion, John went on: "And now think of this: 'He was led as a lamb to the slaughter; as a sheep before her shearers is speechless, so he opened not his mouth.' Who may this be? But let us hear more: 'He was oppressed and afflicted; by oppression and judgment they did away with him unjustly; he was cut off from the land of the living; he poured out his soul in death.' "

A surge of movement went through the company as everyone seemed at once to turn to everyone else, but no one spoke. As John appeared to search for words next to say, James, it seemed, could restrain himself no longer. "Oh, friends," he said, "are we hearing this? Are we remembering? Having lately seen what we have seen and heard what we have heard of him we follow, could any one of us write a more accurate description of him than this ancient prophet wrote?"

To this question there was no answer. Instead, from a far corner of the room came a voice I did not identify: "The prophet's vision, then, was not so much of a people as it was of a person?"

"So it appears," replied James.

"And we know the person, do we not?" I believe it was Thomas who offered this.

Another: "Piece by piece, the pattern comes together; truth by truth, we find what we seek."

Then came a woman's voice: "Oh, how good is God! How gracious to lead us so! How generous to give so much! We thought Jesus a rabbi and we called him Lord. Then we knew him to be the Messiah, the Christ, the Savior, and now at last, this."

It was Joanna who thus spoke, standing as she was a little apart with several of the women, among these that finely crafted lady of Magdala, the seeker Ashabel.

"I have found him!" said Ashabel, her voice vibrant with feeling. "I wish all to know that I have found him! I narrowly missed him at the Damascus Gate the day they took him forth to die. But now I have found him. Or perhaps it is he who has found me. It was by way of a cross he came. Had I met him at the city gate that day, and only there, I would have known him only as he was. Now I know him as he is. And I thank God for all of you!"

As the radiant Ashabel was lovingly embraced by the women around her, a tide of joy swept over the room. Then arose in song the voice of Anna, wife of Reuben, others joining as the psalm unfolded:

Praise the Lord;
Praise the name of the Lord;
Give praise, O servants of the Lord;
You who stand in the house of the Lord,
In the courts of the house of our God...

The psalm concluded, Simon Peter said, "Yes, God be praised, and let our sister Ashabel be thanked. We owe much to her, I believe. It was in large part a question of hers that launched us on a quest for answers we did not have. How tragic when a pilgrim inquires the way and we who should know stammer over our words or stand dumb in our ignorance."

As Peter hesitated momentarily, and as it appeared that some other was about to speak, he lifted a hand calling for silence, then said, "Allow me, please, to go on a little. There is a thing I urgently need to say to you. Something deep within me demands it. If you remember, there was another by whose honest question we were disturbed and stirred, the Roman, Marcus Gracian. I wish now to let you know of a firm resolve of mine: If I am able ever to go to Rome, I shall do all within my power to find this Roman and share with him, as I know them now, the marvels and meanings of our Lord."

Of course, Peter did indeed later go to Rome. There is a belief amongst our people that in Rome Peter searched until at length he located the aged soldier, discovering to his great joy that the man had sometime earlier found the Christ.

There is also the belief amongst us that Marcus Gracian was for many years an ardent follower of our Lord, a powerful witness for him, and a devoted and beloved member of the community of disciples in Rome.

The belief, virtually a tradition now, also holds that the venerable centurion, almost a century old, was one of the first put to death in Nero's evil rampage, dying for him whom he himself had crucified.

Well, at the room on this day, his fellow disciples were both pleased and much moved by Peter's declaration concerning the centurion. Any conversation about it was foreshortened, however, for precisely as he concluded, a stirring among the people near the doorway denoted some unusual activity there. The activity was, in a way, the answer to a prayer: Micah son of Urial had returned.

He was alone. In every aspect of his appearance he bore signs of distress, yet superimposed over all these was a serenity that spoke of peace within. As conversation ceased and all eyes turned to him, he responded simply and sincerely, "Forgive me, my friends; please forgive me."

There was an instant rush of men, as from every side the disciples came to greet and embrace him, a chorus of voices all together saying a single joyous thing: Welcome, Micah. While some did not respond in this way, most did.

Micah was young, about the age of John, perhaps a little younger. He had no sisters or brothers, his mother was long deceased, and his father, a widely known Perean stonecutter and sculptor, had died the previous year. Soon after his father's death, Jesus and the apostles had passed through Perea, and Micah had found among the disciples a refuge from his loneliness. Heavily dependent on others, far more a follower than a leader, he was a reticent type of fellow, not highly self-confident and never given to much speaking.

Now, however, he desired to speak and by his speech he both surprised and pleased all who heard him. He said, "I am so sorry. I hope you can forgive me. And as I have come to know you, I believe you can. I offer no excuse for what I did. I heard the wrong voices; I followed the wrong leader. I know this now. And I think I knew it yesterday when I walked away. Yet I did walk away. Why? I cannot say. Why would anyone ever do the lesser thing when he well knows the greater is better? Why choose to follow a Jonas Ben Eban when Christ is calling? I do not know; perhaps you can tell me. I think I have thought more since yesterday than in all my life before. And certainly I have felt more things more deeply. I desire that you know this: I am resolved now to follow the Lord wherever he leads and never to walk away. I want to walk with you."

The time of rejoicing that followed was only a prelude to all that came after in the life of this young man. For him, this proved a door of transformation that opened upon great avenues of bold adventuring in the Faith. For more than forty of the years after, Christ had in this disciple a faithful and fruitful witness among the people of Media, Parthia, and the Persis.

Now, in the room, however, another concern weighed heavily on many. "What of Jonas Ben Eban? What can you tell us of him?" asked one.

Micah replied, "I can tell you only what he himself has told me. First of all, he is gone. Secondly, he was never with us, not truly."

After further discussion, Matthias said, "It appears we have a mystery here. Why would a man attach himself to this fellowship, pretending an interest, a loyalty, and a commitment he does not have? Clearly, Ben Eban did this. I, for one, do not understand it."

There were in fact none who understood it. And there were some who voiced a concern best expressed by James son of Alphaeus: "Is this perhaps a thing we may be troubled by again and again as time goes on?"

Reflectively Thomas responded, "As time goes on... As time goes on... I have lately thought much of this. Future time. I am sure it has been somewhat in all our minds. For us of this discipleship, my friends, what lies ahead?"

For the space of a few moments, an utter stillness prevailed in the room as disciples all around, each in the private world within, confronted the question many had pondered but of which none had spoken. None had cared to; perhaps none had dared to.

Here they were, many of them already three full years away from their occupations, their homes, and their families. These present days were an interval time; they knew this. But it is the nature of intervals to end, and this one would. The waiting would one day be over.

What then? Would they be able to say farewell to one another and go home? Would they be able to resume their normal lives in the familiar scenes of their communities and the comfort of their homes? Would they be able to declare an episode ended and go back to their fishing and gardening and shopkeeping?

Deeply, many knew that for them this could never happen. Yet none, I think, had been willing to accept the reality of it. But now, for the first time, they would. A penetrating and far-reaching exchange of thoughts ensued.

One launched it, saying, "Let us remember a word of Jesus, actually the final thing many of us ever heard him say: 'You shall be witnesses here, and everywhere, and to the very ends of the earth.' Whatever else may be in our future, I think this is."

Quickly another added: "I am remembering a similar thing he said: 'In me there is good news for all the world; go into all the world, therefore, and carry it to all people everywhere.' "

Another voice picked up the thought and carried it forward: "And 'Make disciples of all nations.' This he has enjoined us to do."

"I have a question," said Joseph Barsabas. "If all go to the ends of the earth, what of Galilee and Samaria and Judea? While some may seek strangers in Spain or Egypt or India, may there not be others who can live out their discipleship among neighbors and family and friends? A woman bearing a water jar — may she not also bear witness for our Lord? I think she may."

Then John offered: "So what lies ahead? We do not entirely know. Nor need we know. But I do believe we know this, and knowing this is enough: Wherever we shall go, whatever we shall do, we shall be first of all disciples."

Simon Peter then put forward a question: "My brothers and sisters, are we ready?"

It was Thomas who replied, speaking for most I am sure: "I believe I am willing, but am I able?"

Another promptly pursued the thought: "Behold us; we are but common people. Who are we with our simple words to assault the world's great citadels of power and centers of learning? And for all that, who are we, having so great a message to deliver, to approach even the most humble with it?"

It was Simon Peter who answered: "Do we not know that if our Lord has a load for us to lift, he knows precisely how heavy that load is and precisely how strong we are? And besides, are we not sure that he lives? And if living, where would he most likely be? With us, I think, with us who love him and who would honor and serve him. And let us not overlook the prophetic promise; God is saying: 'I will pour out my spirit, even on servants and handmaidens, and old men shall dream dreams and the young see visions.' "

John responded: "And we of this place and circumstance may be among those who dream the great dreams and see the far visions. Why not?"

At last, the sun having been a good while set, Simon Peter said to all, "As we say farewell to the day and to one another, please allow a suggestion. In prayer tonight, let each test his or her spirit with this question: Does my Lord have my consent to follow as he leads?"

Seeing images of life uprooted and never again to be the same, the disciples moved away into the night. As would be later evident, the night was a time of hard struggle for some. Fulfilling their discipleship would in some instances require a corresponding commitment of wives, children, parents, and others. With some, loyalty seemed to conflict with loyalty and love with love. For many, the issues were profound, and for many, the night was long.

XI

First to say a truly notable thing on what eventuated as a very significant day was Mary of Bethany, younger daughter of Joseph Eldan of that city. After others had spoken of the bright and agreeable morning, and pleasantries had been passed generally about, she demurely asked permission to address the company.

This was the ninth day, and I believe the only day of the ten on which I heard the sound of Mary's voice. Mary was a beautiful woman, small of stature and features, discreet and well-poised, always of neat appearance and always modest. Now as she spoke, she was heard with the full attention of all. Her message, calmly and pleasantly delivered, was this: "Can anyone doubt that Jesus has done many good things? Among these is this beautiful thing he has done for womanhood. All know that in law, religion, and social custom the world has always been dominated by men. But consider what Jesus has done. From the very first, he welcomed us women into this discipleship. He seemed always to see us as whole persons and worthy in our own merit. I think that in attitude and action Jesus elevated womanhood to a level of equality with men. I think that if the way of Jesus may prevail, never again need a woman feel of herself as a necessary auxiliary to men in a man's world. In the roster of the new that Jesus has brought into the world, include this."

Turning to others of the women who stood nearby, Mary added, "I suppose my sisters see this as I do and are as thankful as I am."

The response was instant and overwhelming. Women closed in from all sides, embracing and kissing the young woman of Bethany, their approbation murmured by some and virtually shouted by others.

Among the men, none could deny the truth of Mary's speech. The attitude of Jesus toward womanhood had been indeed as Mary said, radically novel among the sons of Israel and perhaps among all peoples of the world.

First among the men to speak was Matthew. Calmly but with the intensity of profound feeling, he said, "I thank our sister for her observation. Her words are well spoken and truthful. I am pleased she has spoken. Her speech provides for me an occasion to confess a fault I should have confessed long before. During most of these many months, I inwardly resented the inclusion of women in this discipleship."

As one person, the whole company skipped a breath or two. There was shock in hearing this from Matthew, so level and well-tempered was he. He continued: "So very unlike anything I had known lifelong, the inclusion of women seemed inappropriate somehow. Over time, gradually and sometimes painfully, I struggled my way to acceptance and then to thoroughgoing gratitude. Today I am wholly at peace about it. But I want you to know that I was a long while resentful. Of course, I could not argue with Jesus and I deeply knew that he was right. But within me there was a stubborn resistance that now grieves me greatly. I hope all can forgive me, especially my sisters."

As though certain of the feeling of his fellows, it was in an almost lighthearted way that Matthew spoke, and in further conversation there were other confessions not unlike Matthew's. Among the women, also, there were those who spoke of tension and resentment. It was Joanna who at one instance spoke of the past as a time of growing, and it was it was Joseph Barsabas who added, "And outgrowing what was is like the worm that sunders its outmoded shell to spread wings for flying — painful at times, I should think."

Discussion of the male-female issue soon drifted into conversation concerning other aspects of relationship within the company. Older men admitted earlier resentment of the young. One or two mentioned early misgivings about the youthfulness of even Jesus. Also certain Judean disciples had held at this time or that a partially concealed animosity against those they considered the Galilean cadre.

But now, these old sores healed, they were discussed without rancor, in a spirit of mutual appreciation, and often with smiles. Many of those present spoke freely of rough places along the roads they had traveled. They appeared actually to enjoy the sharing. As mature persons may look back with amusement on the fledgling ways of childhood and youth, so it was among these disciples as they reflected on the process through which they had come.

When one has climbed a mountain, I suppose there is a certain satisfaction in standing atop it and scanning the trail by which he came. And when more than one have climbed together, they will feel the nearer to one another when they can stand at the summit and contemplate the cliffs and crags they overcame on their way.

So it was with the disciples of Jesus on this day. A spirit of comity was upon them, a drawing together, each feeling I think that he or she might reach out and at once embrace all the others. A warmth of fellow-feeling swept over them, a compelling sense of belonging to one another.

After all, I suppose, if each in loyalty and love belonged to the Lord Christ, then in loyalty and love did not each belong to every other? Ultimately, I think, here was the bond that bound them.

It was a joyous time, and it was in the spirit of that joy that Simon the Zealot remarked, looking back over the road by which they had come, "God is really trying to make something of us, isn't he?"

Quickly Nathanael responded: "For me, your comment, Simon, comes as a small providence — it provides the perfect introduction for a small story I wish to tell."

At this there were smiles and chuckles here and there,

and Nathanael responded with a smile of his own. Then he continued: "Today as Philip and I approached this place, we passed the smith's only a short distance away. The smith was at his anvil, and the forge burned hot with the fire he needed. We paused a while and observed the man as he went about his work. With great force he laid hammer to iron and with great skill he shaped it. As the iron cooled, he placed it in the fire again and then again and again.

"As we watched we wondered what the thing on which he worked would turn out to be. But the smith seemed to know. And so he did, for at length we saw that he had made a spade. And when by its shape he was pleased precisely, he plunged it into cold, clear water to temper it. He had made a tool that a gardener might use to turn and till the soil so that flowers and fruits may grow.

"And this is the thought that came to me: God has us on his anvil. Heating and hammering and tempering, he knows what he seeks to make. And whatever that is, if he may succeed, I for one will be content."

"So will we all, of this I am confident." It was Simon Peter who said this.

Well, it was near the fifth hour, and until now John had not arrived. It was rare that he should be away so long. But in the joyous tenor of the day, few if any had thought much of it.

Now John came, and as Nathanael had had an experience to speak about, John had another: "Alone, I walked today atop the city wall. The sun had not yet arisen when I climbed the stair at David's Gate and turned toward the east. Ahead of me, still wrapped in the shadows of the pre-dawn dark, loomed the temple's enormous form. As the slow dawn brought the greater light, I looked upon the city, the homes where people live, the streets where people move, and the shops and mills where they labor. It is the city Jesus loved and over which once we saw him weep.

"Atop the city wall, I walked eastward and then northward toward the temple. Yonder, beyond the wall, lay the Kidron, and beyond the valley Mount Olive's summit in clear outline against the sky. As all things slowly brightened in preparation for the day, I stood and watched the dawn. As the sun's upper arc appeared above the rim of Olivet, rays of light illuminated the temple's towers, then crept downward as the sun climbed up. At last, the valley lay before me bathed in light, and there I saw Gethsemane.

"I remembered then the many times when we and our Lord had taken respite there. And I thought again of that one last time, near the midnight hour, when he walked from us alone into the garden shadows, and we heard this one last time his voice in prayer.

"I thought of the way they came to take him then, and my thought carried me forward through all that came about until the dawn of the next first day. Suddenly it came to me: Today a new week begins. This very day is a first day; today is a resurrection day! It is a day of possibility and promise, a day of new hope, new life. This day, my dear friends, this very day — it is a day for rejoicing and celebration!"

There were shouts: "Praise God!" "How great is the Lord!" "He lives!" "This is the day the Lord has made!"

After a brief interval, for the second time during these days, John climbed onto a chair. Calling for attention, he then said, "Allow me, if I may, to add one thing more. I think that forever hereafter all first days must be counted as singular among days. By his rising, our Lord has forever hallowed the beginning day of every week for as long as time shall last. Forever hereafter, as we journey through the years of our lives, let us be reminded week by week that we do not go alone. He lives! Let us celebrate his life — and ours!"

By John's remarkable declaration many were moved to tears, but these were tears of joy. All the company was caught up and carried on a crest of exultation. There were embraces and kisses, there were songs and prayers, and heaven was surely pleased by the adoration and praise that arose from Jotham's house on this day.

As it would develop, this event was the first of the weekly celebrations that continue to our present time. Whatever the circumstances, and wherever disciples may have been, they have been diligent to gather in groups for fellowship and prayer and praise on the first day of each new week. It is the Lord's Day.

With the hostility that ever increases toward our people, we have been less welcome for seventh day worship in the synagogues. Therefore, our first day gatherings have become more important and precious to us.

It has ever been our understanding that we are a fellowship people. There is so much that may stand against us; therefore, we have a deep need for standing together. Nor is it only that we are forced together by pressures from without; even more are we drawn together by compulsions from within. We have been long convinced that our Lord Christ anticipated our need for one another, and that he was mindful of this when he enjoined the first disciples to tarry together a while in the city of Jerusalem. I think he knew that we would discover something there, and I think we did.

On that week's first day, now 53 years ago, the astute and perceptive James son of Zebedee uttered a truly prophetic word. Following the celebration stirred by John's dramatic narrative, James said: "How precious and productive for us has been our time in these days at this place. Could any one of us alone have come half so far as all of us have come together? Nine days ago, or 49, suppose we had dispersed: each going a separate way, never to meet again? What then?

"Here we have found, I think, the great worth of community. And blessed discovery this is! This that we have found may neither we nor any other ever lose."

On this day, as evening came I observed my Uncle Thaddaeus standing alone on the terrace, his hands at rest on the westward parapet, gazing pensively across the Hinnom into a magnificent sunset that spread its Elysian glow over half the sky. As I approached, he said, "How many sunsets more until that which will happen will happen?" I believe he spoke more to himself than to me.

Another approaching also heard. This was Simon the Zealot. Joining my uncle at the parapet, he replied, "If I know your meaning, great heart, I believe I share the feeling. For me, waiting is not easy. All that is within me resists it; something cries out for a chance to be doing."

Thaddaeus reached out an arm, put it around the Zealot's shoulders, and drew the man to him, saying, "Simon, my friend, you speak of doing? No one has done more in these days than you have done. If this were a journey we were on, no one would have come farther than you. And one day when the waiting is past, none of us will be more ready than you for whatever is next."

By this time a number of others had gathered about, one of these now saying, "Waiting is most difficult, I think, when, as now, one does not know when it will end or how."

Another added thoughtfully, "If it is with anticipation we wait for what we desire and with apprehension we wait for what we dread, is it then with a mixing of these that we wait for the unknown?"

Philip, having just joined the group, responded, "Or may there be perhaps a better way of waiting? I think there is. Surely there is for us of this Faith and fellowship. It is for a promise of our Lord that we wait, and I trust him. If I may know and trust the giver, then I can surely trust the gift. Indeed, it is with anticipation that I wait. But, you see, anticipation of the desirable is itself desirable, and who should grow weary of this or fret from the length of waiting?"

"Look!" called someone, "behold the sunset!"

By now, virtually all were on the terrace, and of those

not already so engaged, most turned at once to face the west. There they looked upon a magnificence beyond the power of any language to describe.

The Elysian glow that had overspread all the western sky had now converged low above the hills beyond Hinnom. There the sun's last rays had spent themselves, bestowing all their remaining light on tiered layers of springtime cloud.

Ever changing and slowly fading, the magnificent scene sent forth its serenity and its beauty to these scores of up-welling hearts hungrily reaching out to meet it.

On the terrace, a solemn hush held all within its power. Then arose a voice, whose I have never known:

The heavens are proclaiming the glory of God,
The sky displays the artistry of his hand;
Day after day, the days tell of his majesty,
Night after night declares him yet to be.
Their speech is without word,
And there is no sound for the ear,
Yet their voice goes out through all the earth
And their message is heard to the ends of the world.

The voice died away and there was stillness again. Then someone said, "God speaks in many ways. However, what he says in the beauty of a sunset, glorious as it may be, will henceforth serve mostly as a reminder of the greater thing he has said and the greater beauty he has shown in the person and presence of Jesus our Lord."

Gradually the dimming light surrendered to the pervading dark and night had come.

Then came a voice, the same as before I think, but a voice not known to me: "If the sun goes down, it will rise again. Therefore let every sunrising speak forth this greatest truth: He lives."

After this the disciples, by singles and by twos and threes, slowly drifted away. They were near an hour going. Peter,

John, Matthias, and Joseph Barsabas remained at the room. As the four moved inside from the terrace, I heard Peter remark, "This has been a remarkable day."

XII

It was the morning of the tenth day. An hour before the sunrising, the city lay enwrapped in that singular stillness that seems always to precede a dawn. Under that expectant hush the world seems always to hold its breath for a while, as though anticipating the revelations that may come with light.

So was it now. All was still, no wind stirred, and the finches and larks had not yet awakened to salute daybreak with their song.

Wrapped against the early chill, disciples made their way through streets yet dark and climbed to the rooftop of Jotham's house. As they began to assemble here, the four within the room arose, lit the lamps, and commenced preparation for the day. Before the first gray sign of dawn appeared above Olivet, at least four score of the disciples had come.

Why had they come so early? They had felt themselves drawn, some said. Others said that having yesterday seen the sun set, they wished today to see it rise, although they were unable to say precisely why.

Never, by day or night during the whole of the ten days, had there been fewer than four or five at the room. Usually by day there had been forty or fifty. But today, before the sunrise, there were more than five score, the major portion of whom were gathered on the terrace.

There were conversations, all these in tones of reverence, subdued as though spoken in the precincts of a holy place. There were torches and lamps, only a few, but enough nonetheless to create eerie effects of light and shadow on garments and faces among all the assembled company. There was that sense of nearness one with another that may come when a deep, silent darkness surrounds and seems to press in from every side.

It was a long while before the dark above Olivet began to show signs of dawn. But then it did, and at length the great sun broke clearly into view, unveiling a sky of unbroken blue. There was no cloud, no spectacle, only nature's sovereign orb arising from beyond the temple towers. On the terrace the torches and lamps were one by one extinguished, and this company of the Lord's people settled in for yet another day.

There was much joy — theirs a joy not dependent on the beauty of a sunrise. James son of Zebedee presided for morning prayers, reading passages from the great prophet:

> *Hear this now, O Jacob,*
> *My servant Israel whom I have chosen;*
> *This is the promise of the Lord who made you:*
> *I will pour water on the thirsty land*
> *And my spirit upon your children.*
> *They shall spring up like grass amid the waters,*
> *Like willows by flowing streams.*
> *I have redeemed you, O Israel;*
> *I have swept away your transgressions like a cloud,*
> *Your sins like a mist.*
> *Sing, O heavens, for it is the Lord who has done this!*
> *Shout, O deep places of the earth,*
> *Break forth in song, all you mountains,*
> *You forests and all trees,*
> *For the Lord has redeemed you*
> *And will be glorified in the earth.*

Prayers were characterized by great thanksgivings, and afterward there were many who expressed to others deep gratitude for helpfulness given and fellowship shared. In the room, on the terrace, and about the stair, pairs and small groups were variously clustered in conversation.

What next occurred has since been often reviewed and relived by all who experienced it. Years afterward, in a gathering of disciples, as they spoke of it, I once heard Joseph Barsabas say, "Do you know how it is when you feel eyes upon you and you are compelled to turn to see whose? Suppose, when you turn, no one is there? And suppose you strongly feel that there has been a call for silence and no one has spoken?"

Well, first there was the silence. It came upon all, person by person, falling first on one and then another. The murmur of voices slowly waned, ebbing until at last all were still, no person knowing why. It was as though someone had indeed called for silence, only no one had.

Where within the group the silence began no one ever knew. But somewhere one or two or a few felt it first — a subtle sense that any sound was discordant, inappropriate somehow.

It was as though from somewhere the silence had come, and the silence was real, and sound of any sort would be an intrusion upon it. Those who felt it left off their speaking, listening as though the silence itself must first be heard.

Throughout the company the phenomenon spread, until at last all had entered into the silence and all were still. For long moments it was so. At length, brows furrowed with perplexity and great questions showing in their eyes, there were some who turned one to another or searchingly peered about. There were a few who whispered to others: "What is it, do you think?" Not knowing, those questioned shook their heads and silently turned away.

Then, so it seemed, there arose a gentle wind. Although from sunrise the day was calm, there was the wind, if wind it really was. There was indeed a quiet stirring of the air, though not passing as is the way of winds, but circulating as whirlwinds do, although not in a single direction apparently, but seemingly moving in all directions at once. And the wind was warm, not cool as most winds are, its touch like a caress and warm upon the flesh.

Presently, as quietly as it came, the wind diminished and died away. But the warmth remained, as did the silence. Then came the Great Excitement, with all that followed and yet follows.